Has being on a gluten-free diet made you feel like you have to settle for mediocre imitations of your favorite foods? Be prepared for a wonderful surprise!

With Dr. Jeri's gluten-free cookbook you'll never again have to settle for food that's "almost as good as the real thing." Now you can enjoy moist, flavorful cakes, fluffy biscuits and cookies that rival the ones Grandma used to bake.

Try Dr. Jeri's gluten-free recipes and soon you'll be saying, "I can't believe it's gluten-free. It's delicious!"

Books by Jeri Mills, M.D.

Tapestry of Healing

Healing is Believing

Gluten-Free with Dr. Jeri

Gluten-Free
With Dr. Jeri

Delicious Meals and Decadent Desserts

Jeri Mills, M.D.

White Sage Press

Readers may contact the publisher at

White Sage Press
Jeri@JeriMillsMD.com

Cover design by Jeri Mills
Photographs by Jeri Mills

ISBN 978-0-9713350-4-2

Library of Congress Control Number:
2103950519

Printed in the United States of America
October 2013
10 9 8 7 6 5 4 3 2 1

*For all the people who
encouraged me to write this book.*

Table of Contents

Soups

Main Dishes

Side Dishes

Crepes: Savory and Sweet

Acknowledgements

I'd like to thank my friends Anita Kindt, Penny Leisch, Yoly Fivas and Alta Arnold who helped proof-read this manuscript.

If it were not for Phil Ball's unending patience when he taught me to use Photoshop, this book would have no cover. So thank you Phil!

One cannot write a cookbook without the people who are willing to taste the products. And so I must also extend my gratitude to my friends and neighbors as well as the members of the Professional Writers of Prescott and the Prescott Digital Photography Group who were my kind and willing Beta Tasters.

Introduction

When I found out I had to go on a gluten-free diet, I knew that if I were to succeed, it would have to be an exercise in creativity, not a punishment. I started by doing research. First, I read several articles that contained lists of foods to be avoided, as well as a few recipes.

Two things struck me when I read the recipes. Many of the older, more traditional gluten-free baked goods contained combinations of at least five different kinds of flour. That meant there would be a major financial investment before I could even try to make one recipe.

The next observation was that the main ingredient in the more traditional gluten-free recipes was often rice flour. The over-the-counter gluten-free breads, cakes and cookies I tried (mostly rice flour) not only tasted terrible, they were heavy as bricks and acted like cement in my digestive tract. There had to be a better way!

While searching the Internet, I came across a book of almond flour recipes. Now *that* sounded appealing and also much healthier than filling my poor, innocent digestive tract with the gluey horror of rice flour! I ordered the book immediately.

While waiting for my new book to arrive, I did more Internet searches. Along with nutritional information and tips about how to cook with various alternative flours, I found hundreds of almond flour recipes and started trying some of them out. Who ever said you lose weight when you go on a gluten- free diet clearly does not have a love for baking and creative cookery!

Being a "creative home cook," I have rarely found a recipe I didn't think I could improve. I soon found the same to be true of the gluten-free recipes. So I started playing with recipes. At first, I made small adjustments. Then I decided I simply *must* figure out how to transform all my favorite cake and cookie recipes into the gluten-free marvels I knew they could be.

My tasters were my friends and neighbors, the staff at the hospitals where I work, people in classes I attended along with the folks at the local computer club and writers' association. Besides having lots of people to test my recipes, what better way to make new friends than to feed them? When the NON-gluten-free folks in the groups started telling me they didn't care whether there was gluten in my baked goods or not, they were just good, I knew I had succeeded!

Besides being born with an overwhelming need to feed my immediate world, I have always shared recipes with friends, co-workers and patients. In my holistic medical practice, talking about diets to maintain optimal health has always been a priority. Simply telling someone to eat healthy food often goes in one ear and out the other. Showing them how by passing out delicious, easy-to-prepare recipes gives them the tools they need to start making changes. And so, I passed out recipes.

When I had to go on a gluten-free diet, the impetus to share was no different. I had a favorite little patient who suffered from Celiac disease. Her mother was frustrated because she couldn't come up with enough healthy, appealing recipes to satisfy her child. So I brought them a number of my recipes.

When I mentioned what I had done to one of the nurses, she told me that *her* daughter also had Celiac disease and was always looking for new recipes. Of course, I made copies of my recipes for her too. It soon became clear that wherever I went, someone I met was on a gluten-free diet or had a family member who needed to be. So I got into the habit of carrying recipes to every hospital and clinic where I worked, and then shared them with anyone who was interested.

After years of sharing recipes with friends and patients, many have suggested that I write a cookbook. It has taken me four years to create mouth-watering, gluten-free versions of all my favorite foods. When you look through the recipes in this book, you will discover lots of appetizers, salads, soups, main dishes and even a few cookies and muffins that are high protein, high fiber, low glycemic and suitable for most healthy eating regimens, but this is not a diet book. When I set out to create gluten-free versions of my favorite foods the list most definitely included my favorite comfort foods and, as promised in the title, pastries that are delightfully decadent.

I firmly believe that we all need to treat ourselves once in a while. When I lived in New

Mexico, we had a huge community potluck every Sunday. I used the setting to indulge my own love of baking. I ate satisfying and nutritious meals all week, choosing lots of veggies, salads, lean proteins and fruits while I studied cookbooks so that I could come up with the most decadent desserts imaginable for the potlucks. On Sundays, I would have a little of everything that looked good, along with a modest serving of my killer dessert. Not only did I never feel deprived, it was the only time in my adult life that I could fit into size six jeans!

I believe the best way to maintain a restrictive diet is to set aside special times when indulgence is allowed. Telling someone they have to give up one of their favorite pleasures *forever is* a sure way to guarantee failure, but anyone can be sensible for six days!

This does NOT mean you can eat gluten on Sundays. If you're like me, you will have symptoms for a couple weeks each time you cheat. It does mean that even if you have high cholesterol, it's OK to have a single serving of something special once a week or once a month, in order to satisfy your cravings and avoid becoming so frustrated that you just chock up the whole idea of healthy eating.

I tell my patients there is no such thing as cholesterol on Christmas, Thanksgiving and their birthday. I encourage you to set aside special occasions to treat yourself, and when you do, eat the good stuff!

I hope my recipes will satisfy your cravings and help you maintain your gluten-free life style without ever missing what you left behind.

What is Gluten?

Gluten is the protein that makes wheat flour sticky. It helps bread rise and gives it the texture we are accustomed to. It's also a popular thickener for sauces and gravies. Unfortunately, gluten is also a protein that commonly causes allergic reactions in the gastrointestinal tract leading to chronic inflammation which can cause constipation, diarrhea, bloating, cramping and even inadequate absorption of nutrients. In some individuals, the only symptoms may be fatigue or generalized malaise.

Celiac disease is an auto-immune disease that is controlled by eating a gluten-free diet. It is diagnosed with an antibody test. Symptoms of a number of other conditions including Crohn's disease, irritable bowel syndrome and ADHD have been shown to improve with a gluten-free diet, even though the antibody test used to diagnose celiac disease may be negative in those people.

Gluten is found in wheat, barley and rye. Oats may be a problem for two reasons. While oats contain no gluten, they do contain a protein that cross-reacts with gluten in about ten percent of people with gluten sensitivity. For this reason, it is recommended that oats never be fed to children with celiac disease. If gluten sensitive adults wish to eat oats, they should begin by consuming a small amount to see if they experience a recurrence of their symptoms.

The second problem with oats is that they are often contaminated with other gluten-containing grains. That problem can be solved by purchasing oats that have been processed in facilities that are certified gluten-free.

After eliminating gluten from one's diet, it usually takes at least two weeks for the inflammation in the intestinal tract to resolve and for symptoms to begin to abate. In cases where there is severe inflammation, a gastroenterologist may find it necessary to prescribe a course of steroids to bring about initial relief of symptoms.

If you have gluten sensitivity, removing *most* of the gluten from your diet won't relieve your symptoms. We're talking about an allergic reaction, so minute amounts of gluten are enough to cause a problem.

It's simple to remove the obvious sources of gluten from your diet, but removing them all will require *reading the fine print on labels*. Common "hidden" sources of gluten include: beer, soy sauce, bouillon, MSG, salad dressing, sauce on frozen vegetables, soup mixes, malt flavoring, texturized vegetable protein and even many lunch meats and sausages.

If a product is not labeled "gluten-free" and you are still uncertain after reading the label, most companies will provide more detailed information on their web sites. Many will also send you a list of the products they make "without gluten ingredients." If you have a severe sensitivity, this precaution may not be enough. You may have to limit your diet to products that have been made in an environment that is "certified gluten free". That means there have never been any gluten-containing ingredients processed on their equipment.

Happily, more and more commonly used products like soups, salad dressings and frozen dinners are being produced without gluten and manufacturers are labeling the products as such. By simply reading labels and purchasing just a few special ingredients at the grocery store, gluten-free eating can be easy and delicious!

About the Ingredients

After tasting several dense, grainy, rice flour-based cakes and breads that were available at my local grocery store, I was horrified. I knew I had to give up gluten for the rest of my life, but I had no intention of punishing myself by eating tasteless, cardboard imitations of my favorite foods. There had to be better options!

I started my quest by reading dozens of gluten-free recipes. Most contained five or six types of flour, pectin and xanthan gum. Besides having very limited storage space in my tiny kitchen, it seemed like a huge investment to purchase a bunch of products I might not like. Plus, I'm lazy and didn't want to have to deal with so many ingredients. So I kept reading. Finally, I came across a number of recipes that called for almond flour.

I loved the idea of using finely ground almonds instead of flour in my baked goods. Almonds are delicious and they have way more protein, fiber and healthy fats than rice. They also carry the added bonus of being low in carbohydrates.

So I prepared a few almond flour recipes. They tasted better and had a much lighter texture than rice flour based products, but I ran into three problems.

1.) My cookie dough ran all over the pan resulting in cookies that were thin, fragile and extremely unattractive.

2.) The cakes didn't taste bad, but they had a very different texture from those I was accustomed to eating. To me, they just weren't cake.

3.) I still had to find some other product to thicken soups, sauces and gravies.

First, I tried using coconut flour as a thickener for my cakes and cookies. Coconut flour is made from the pulp that remains after most of the oil has been expressed from fresh coconut meat. It's seventy-five percent fiber, so it acts like a sponge, soaking up excess liquid. I thought it would be the perfect way to improve both the texture and nutritional profile of my baked goods. In fact, when I used relatively tiny amounts in my recipes—only one or two tablespoons—it did solve the runny batter problem. Unfortunately, it created two new problems.

1.) Whether I purchased the coconut flour in stores or on line, it had an unpleasant, slightly rancid taste that came through in my foods.

2.) When I added coconut flour to cakes, even in small amounts, the cakes became dense and chewy.

Finally, I decided to play with some of the commercially available gluten-free flour blends. After several disappointing starts, I came across a product called Better Batter Gluten-Free All Purpose Flour. While I did not find it to be the perfect one-to- one substitute for wheat flour in baked goods that it claimed to be, I did find that when I added relatively small amounts to almond flour, I was finally able to achieve the texture, taste and mouth feel I was looking for when I began creating gluten-free versions of my favorite recipes. I also found Better Batter to be an excellent flour substitute for thickening sauces, gravies and creamed soups.

The baked goods in this book require a combination of two products, **blanched almond flour** (this is *not* the same thing as almond meal) and **Better Batter Gluten-Free All Purpose Flour.** Both products are readily available in grocery stores, specialty stores and on line. *(See the list of my favorite sources at the end of this book.)*

I searched the shelves of grocery stores and Wal-Mart stores in all the tiny, rural communities where I have worked in Arizona, Minnesota and Louisiana. With the exception of my two "exotic" flour substitutes, the ingredients in my recipes have been available from those sources.

Because gluten-free flours don't have the "stick" of wheat flour, gluten-free recipes generally require more eggs than traditional recipes. This means that the gluten-free products contain more protein and fat and so have a lower glycemic index than their counterparts. Unfortunately, it also means that they contain more cholesterol. Replacing whole eggs with egg whites or "egg substitute" changes the taste and texture of the baked goods—in a bad way. So, in order to achieve a slightly healthier product, I use omega-3 eggs in my home. Please also note that I have used **extra-large eggs** for the recipes in this book.

I often use yogurt to lighten the texture of my cakes and biscuits. In those recipes I have specified **FAGE 2% Greek yogurt.** If you use a different brand, please *read the label*. The only ingredients should be milk and live culture. If a brand of yogurt contains food starch, gelatin or pectin, it will affect the texture of your baked goods and the "modified food starch" used to thicken some products may not be gluten-free.

If a recipe calls for sour cream, please use a product that contains only cream and live culture like Daisy or Knudson. Again, products containing food starch and gelatin create inferior baked goods. Even when you're using sour cream as a condiment, the real thing tastes better. Whether you buy blends or the real thing, the calorie count is about the same and the price is similar, so love yourself and get the good stuff!

When a recipe calls for butter, always use **unsalted butter.** The perfect amount of salt will be added to the recipe as a separate ingredient.

Let's take a minute to talk about fats and oils. In baking, the less saturated the fat, the lighter the texture. So, for a super light muffin or yellow cake, like the ones Mom (and Duncan Hines) used to bake, I have chosen poly-unsaturated corn oil. In other recipes, where I want to achieve the flavors found in fine restaurants and gourmet bakeries, I use butter—not margarine, *butter.* If you must have a healthier fat profile, using grape seed oil or macadamia nut oil, which both have a pleasant, nutty taste and are high in mono-saturated fats, would be a far better substitute than margarine.

One final technical note: The recipes in this book were developed in my home in Prescott, Arizona where the altitude is 5200 feet. If you live closer to sea level, cooking times will be shorter. So start checking baked goods for doneness after the shortest cooking time in the recipe.

Finally, after years of experimenting in my own kitchen, I am able to offer you a collection of gluten-free versions of all my favorite foods that I believe to be as good as or better than the originals. I hope you love them as much as I do!

Appetizers and Dips

Tzatziki

2 cups Fage 2% Greek yogurt
2 cloves garlic
1/8 teaspoon salt
2 tablespoons dried dill weed
1 English cucumber
1 tablespoon toasted walnut oil

Put the yogurt in a medium sized bowl. Press the garlic through a garlic press then stir it into the yogurt. Add the salt and dill weed then stir to mix thoroughly.

Peel, seed and finely dice the cucumber. Blot it between two paper towels to remove any excess water then mix it with the yogurt and herbs. Cover and refrigerate for at least two hours to allow the flavors to blend. Drizzle walnut oil over the top just before serving.

Serve as a dip with raw veggies or GF chips or as a side to chicken or fish.

Hummus

¼ sweet onion
3-4 cloves garlic
2 cans of garbanzo beans
¼ cup toasted sesame tahini
¼ teaspoon ground cumin
½ teaspoon ground coriander
A dash of cayenne pepper
Salt to taste
1/3 cup olive oil
Zest from one lemon
2-3 tablespoons water
1-2 tablespoons freshly squeezed lemon juice

Drain and rinse the garbanzo beans.

In a food processor, pulse the garlic and onions until they are finely chopped. Add all the remaining ingredients except the lemon juice and purée until smooth. Add one tablespoon of lemon juice and purée. Taste the hummus. Add more lemon juice and salt to taste. If the mixture is too thick, add a little more water and pulse to mix.

Store covered in the refrigerator.

Serve with raw veggies or chips.

Mango Salsa

1 mango – peeled and diced
¾ cup jicama - diced
3 tablespoons sweet onion - finely diced
2 large jalapenos - seeded and finely diced
Leaves of 1 small bunch of cilantro - coarsely chopped
Juice of 1 lime
1 teaspoon olive oil

Mix all the ingredients in a large bowl.

Keeps in the refrigerator for 1-2 days.

A wonderful side for chicken or fish.

Cranberry Salsa

1 pound fresh cranberries
3 Serrano chilies pith and seeds removed
1 tablespoon orange zest
1/3 cup fresh orange juice
1 head of cilantro
1 tablespoon Grand Marnier or orange juice
1 tablespoon fresh ginger root finely grated
1/3 to ½ cup honey to taste
¼ teaspoon orange extract

Cut the chilies into small pieces then put them in a food processor and pulse till fine. Discard the large stems from the cilantro then add it along with the ginger, orange zest, orange juice and Grand Marnier. Pulse till fine. Add the cranberries and pulse until they are coarsely chopped. Turn into a bowl and add honey to taste. Refrigerate at least 6 hours before serving.

Keeps several days in the refrigerator.

For a tangy appetizer, pour over a block of cream cheese and serve with your favorite gluten-free crackers.

Cranberry salsa is also great as a side for turkey, chicken or fish.

To me, it just isn't Thanksgiving without cranberry salsa. I find I always have to make a double recipe because I can't resist tasting it over and over again. If I didn't make lots, there'd be none left for company!

Basil Pesto

2 cloves garlic
2 cups basil leaves
½ cup grated parmesan cheese
¼ to ½ cup olive oil
½ cup pine nuts

In a food processor:
Pulse the garlic till finely chopped then add the basil leaves and pulse till chopped. Add the cheese and pulse to mix. With the food processor turned on, slowly pour in the olive oil until you have achieved the desired consistency. Add the nuts and pulse till they are coarsely chopped and combined with the other ingredients.

Store in a bowl covered with plastic wrap that has been pushed down to adhere to the top of the pesto. Sealing air away from the pesto prevents it from becoming discolored.

Keeps several days in the refrigerator.

To freeze: Add just enough oil for the pesto to become shiny but still remain a thick paste. Freeze in ice cube trays or in single serving sized lumps about half an inch apart in a large zip-lock bag. Thaw just before serving and add olive oil to achieve desired consistency.

Cilantro Pesto

2 cloves garlic
1 head of cilantro
½ cup grated parmesan cheese
¼ to ½ cup olive oil
½ cup raw sunflower seeds

In a food processor:
Pulse the garlic till finely chopped then add the cilantro leaves (discard the thick stems) and pulse till chopped. Add the cheese and pulse to mix. With the food processor turned on, slowly pour in the olive oil until you have achieved the desired consistency. Add the seeds and pulse till they are coarsely chopped and mixed with the other ingredients.

Store in a bowl covered with plastic wrap that has been pushed down to adhere to the top of the pesto. Sealing air away from the pesto prevents it from becoming discolored. Keeps several days in the refrigerator.

To freeze: Add just enough oil for the pesto to become shiny, but still remain a thick paste. Freeze in ice cube trays or in single serving sized lumps about half an inch apart in a large zip-lock bag. Thaw just before serving and add olive oil to achieve desired consistency.

Pesto Dip

1 cup ricotta cheese
½ cup of your favorite pesto
¼ teaspoon salt

Combine the ingredients in a serving bowl.

Serve with raw veggies or chips.

This is also a lovely topping for pasta.

Mushroom Almond Pâté

1 small onion finely diced
2 cloves garlic finely diced
½ stick butter
¾ pound cremini mushrooms sliced
A pinch of dried rosemary
A pinch of dried thyme
1 cup slivered blanched almonds
1 tablespoon walnut or almond oil
Salt and pepper to taste

Lightly toast the almonds at **325° for 3-5 minutes**.

Sauté the onions in butter till they begin to caramelize. Add the garlic, rosemary and thyme then cook for a minute. Add the mushrooms and sauté till they begin to brown and the liquid is evaporated.

Put the almonds in a food processor with the oil and process till creamy. Add the mushroom-onion mixture and pulse till smooth.

Turn into a mold (or a small bowl) lined with plastic wrap, cover and refrigerate.

Remove from the refrigerator 20 minutes before serving time and turn out onto a plate.

Serve with your favorite GF crackers or bread.

Corn Cakes

4 cups of fresh sweet corn (about 5 or 6 ears)
¼ cup chives
3 eggs
2 tablespoons melted butter
¼ cup Better Batter GF flour
1 tablespoon milk
½ teaspoon salt
1 teaspoon sugar
A dash of cayenne
1 teaspoon California chili powder
A dash of garlic powder
2 tablespoons melted butter

Butter to sauté

Purée the chives and half the corn in a blender or food processor. Add the egg, milk, spices and 2 tablespoons melted butter. Mix. Pour into a bowl, add the remaining corn kernels and mix well.

Drop by rounded tablespoon into a buttered non-stick frying pan. Sauté on medium-low heat for 3-4 minutes on each side.

Serve with sour cream and salsa.

Chickpea Flour Pizza

2/3 cup chickpea flour
1/3 teaspoon salt
1 cup water
½ teaspoon finely chopped dried rosemary*
3 tablespoons extra-virgin olive oil
2-3 cloves of garlic finely chopped
1 tablespoon sun dried tomato finely diced
5 kalamata olives finely chopped
1 tablespoon sweet onion finely chopped
3 tablespoons freshly grated Parmesan

Mix the chickpea flour, salt and rosemary in a bowl. Slowly add the water, whisking constantly until smooth. **Let the batter sit for 30 minutes**.

Heat 1 tablespoon of olive oil in a 12-inch nonstick frying pan. Stir the batter once then pour it into the pan. Drizzle the remaining olive oil on top. Cook over medium heat until the bottom is golden and crisp and the top is almost set. Turn and cook until the second side is brown.

Turn the pizza onto a baking sheet and sprinkle the onion, garlic and olives over the top.

Broil 1-2 minutes. Then put the parmesan cheese on top and **broil until melted**, about a minute. Cut into wedges and serve hot.

*Use a coffee grinder to grind the dried rosemary into a fine powder.

Crab Cheesecake

10½ ounces cream cheese
2 eggs
½ cup sour cream
1 tablespoon freshly squeezed lemon juice
3 tablespoons onion
1/8 teaspoon cayenne
¼ teaspoon garlic powder
1 tablespoon dried dill weed
¼ teaspoon sweet paprika
1 pound lump or claw crabmeat *(Pasteurized, refrigerated crab meat is surprisingly good.)*

1 pretzel crumb crust

Allow the cream cheese to come to room temperature. Combine the cream cheese, eggs, and sour cream then mix at **low** speed till blended. *(You don't want to beat a lot of air in this one or the cheesecake will crack).*

Press the onion through a garlic press. Discard the solid chunks and use only the juice that comes out. Add the lemon juice, onion juice and herbs to the cheese mixture and beat to combine. Fold in the crabmeat. Pour the mixture into a cooled pretzel crumb crust in an eight-inch spring form pan.

Bake at 350° for 50 minutes
To test for doneness, gently nudge the pan. If the center still jiggles, it's not done.

Wait at least 30 minutes before removing the sides of the spring form pan.

Serve warm as an appetizer with crackers or as a main dish with a salad or fruit.

Pretzel Crumb Crust

2 cups gluten-free pretzels crushed into crumbs
¾ stick butter

Mix the pretzel crumbs together in a bowl.

Place a sheet of parchment paper over the bottom of a eight-inch spring form pan then attach the sides. The sides will hold the parchment paper in place. Trim the edges of the paper that are sticking out from the pan.

Butter the bottom and sides of the pan then press the pretzel mixture into the pan covering the bottom and the sides. Place the spring form pan on a baking sheet.

Bake at 350° for 10 minutes.

Onion Tart

3 sweet onions
¼ teaspoon salt
3 tablespoons olive oil
½ cup oil packed, julienned sundried tomatoes
drained
4 ounces fresh goat cheese

Cream Cheese Crust

Prepare the dough for the crust and refrigerate.

Cut the onions into thin slices and sauté in the olive oil over medium heat until they are caramelized to a dark brown.

In the meantime, dust the dough with almond flour and roll between two sheets of parchment paper till it's about 3/8 inch thick. Turn the dough onto a non-stick tart pan. Fit it into the pan then cut the excess from the top. Pierce the crust with a fork to prevent it from bubbling.

Bake at 350° for 12-14 minutes until it just begins to brown.

Spread the onions evenly over the cooked crust. Evenly distribute the tomatoes on top then dot with the goat cheese.

Bake at 350° for 15-20 minutes till the veggies are warmed through and the cheese is melted.

Cream Cheese Crust

1/3 cup butter
2 ounces cream cheese
¼ teaspoon salt
½ teaspoon sugar
½ cup + 2 tablespoons Better Batter GF flour
½ cup + 3 tablespoons blanched almond flour
3 tablespoons cold water
Extra almond flour for rolling out dough

Place the dry ingredients in a food processor and pulse until well mixed. Dice the COLD butter and cream cheese and add to the food processor. Pulse a couple times until the dough looks like peas. Add the water and pulse a couple times. Turn the dough into a bowl and kneed once or twice with your hands till the dough just comes together. Wrap the dough in plastic wrap and refrigerate it for at least two hours or overnight.

Polenta Bites

1 recipe polenta
1 cup balsamic vinegar
¼ cup olive oil
4 ounces sliced mozzarella cheese*
½ cup basil pesto
1 pint cherry tomatoes cut in half

Prepare the polenta as directed. Cut it into half-inch slices then cut each slice in half. Brush with olive oil then broil on a **low rack** for 2-3 minutes on each side till they are golden-brown.

Put the balsamic in a small sauce pan and simmer over medium heat until the volume reduces by 2/3 and you have a thick sauce. Cool. *(This can be done a day ahead.)*

Cut the mozzarella slices the size of the polenta squares. Put a piece of cheese on top of each polenta square then broil for 30-60 seconds until the cheese is melted.

Top each square with a half teaspoon of pesto and a tomato half. Drizzle with the balsamic reduction.

*For extra flavor, substitute smoked fontina or smoked mozzarella cheese.

Polenta

4 cups water
1 tablespoon butter
¼ teaspoon salt
1 cup yellow corn meal
1 cup grated parmesan cheese
¼ cup grated Romano cheese

Put the water, butter and salt in a 3 quart sauce pan. Heat over high heat until it comes to a boil. Slowly add the corn meal, a little at a time while whisking constantly to prevent lumps from forming. Cook over low heat stirring constantly with a pancake turner until the mixture is extremely thick, **about 20 minutes.** Then stir in the cheese.

Transfer to an 8½ inch loaf pan that has been lined with plastic wrap. Cover with plastic wrap. Allow the polenta to cool to room temperature.

Refrigerate for at least 6 hours, up to four days.

Mini Mushroom Turnovers

cream cheese crust (recipe follows)

½ large onion finely diced (one cup raw)
8 ounces fresh cremini mushrooms
2 tablespoons butter
½ tablespoon olive oil
1 clove garlic finely minced
A pinch of dried rosemary
Salt to taste

Egg wash:
1 egg
1 tablespoon water

Prepare the pastry at least two hours, up to one day ahead and refrigerate.

Filling:
Sauté the onions in a tablespoon of butter and the olive oil over medium-low heat until they caramelize to a dark brown. Put the onions in a dish. Add one more tablespoon of butter to the pan then add the mushrooms, garlic and rosemary. Sauté over medium heat until they are soft and the water has evaporated. Salt at the end of cooking. Mushrooms get tough if you salt them right away.

Combine the onions and mushrooms in a food processor and pulse till they are well mixed and finely chopped. Set the filling aside.

Assembly:

Roll the dough between two pieces of parchment paper using extra almond flour to keep it from sticking till it's about 3/16 inch thick. Cut into 3½ inch circles *(I use the rim of a wine glass.)* Separate out each round of dough then put the scraps together, roll them again and keep making circles till you have used up all the dough.

To fill, place about 1 teaspoon of filling over half of the circle leaving about 3/8 inch near the edge uncovered. Fold the unfilled side over the top and gently pinch around the edge to seal the two cut ends.

Lay the little half circle pockets at least a half inch apart on a parchment-lined cookie sheet. Cut several small slits in the top of each crescent to serve as air vents.

Beat the egg and water together to make an egg wash. Brush the top of each pastry with egg wash.

Bake at 400° for 16-20 minutes till golden brown. Serve immediately.

Makes 16 tarts

These are a bit labor intensive, but the filling and the crust can be made a day or two ahead and refrigerated. They can be assemble a couple hours in advance and refrigerated.
Just pop them into the oven when you're about ready to serve. They're definitely worth the effort!

Cream Cheese Crust

1/3 cup butter
2 ounces cream cheese
¼ teaspoon salt
½ teaspoon sugar
½ cup + 2 tablespoons Better Batter GF flour
½ cup + 3 tablespoons blanched almond flour
3 tablespoons cold water
Extra almond flour for rolling out dough

Place the dry ingredients in a food processor and pulse until well mixed. Dice the COLD butter and cream cheese and add to the food processor. Pulse a couple times until the dough looks like peas. Add the water and pulse a couple times. Turn the dough into a bowl and kneed once or twice with your hands till the dough just comes together. Wrap the dough in plastic wrap and refrigerate it for at least two hours or overnight.

Chicken Fingers

¼ cup almond flour
2 tablespoons finely grated parmesan cheese
Garlic powder to taste
1 teaspoon tomato-basil-garlic flavor Mrs. Dash
1 egg
1 tablespoon water
12 chicken tenderloins
Grape seed or olive oil to sauté

Trim the white membrane from the chicken pieces.

Combine the almond flour, cheese and spices in a flat dish. Beat the egg and water together in a shallow, wide-mouthed bowl. Dip the chicken in egg wash then roll it in the flour-cheese-spice mixture.

Sauté over medium-low heat for about 4-5 minutes on each side till the chicken is cooked through.

Serves 4

Spicy Praline Pecans

1/3 cup brown sugar
3 tablespoons water
½ teaspoon hot chili powder
A few dashes of cayenne pepper
2 teaspoons vanilla
¼ teaspoon salt
3 tablespoons butter
3 cups pecan halves

Cook the sugar and water in a large frying pan over medium heat until it's bubbly. Add the chili powder, pepper, salt, vanilla and butter. Mix well then add the nuts and stir continuously to coat. Cook until the nuts are warm and beginning to release their flavors (about 5-7 minutes). Stir frequently so they don't burn. Spread the nuts on a foil or parchment lined baking sheet to cool.

Salads

Spinach and Fresh Fruit Salad

6 cups baby spinach
2 cups strawberries
2 kiwis
1 orange
4 hard-boiled eggs
1 cup walnut halves
1 cup crumbled feta or blue cheese

Slice 1 cup of strawberries and toss with the spinach then divide it between 4 dinner plates.

Cut the remaining strawberries in half.
Peel and slice the kiwis and the oranges.
Quarter the eggs lengthwise.

Top each dish of spinach and sliced berries with the strawberry halves, kiwi slices, orange slices, walnuts and cheese then top with fresh raspberry vinaigrette.

Raspberry Vinaigrette

2 cups fresh or frozen raspberries
2 tablespoons water
2 tablespoons white balsamic vinegar
4 teaspoons sugar
A dash of salt
½ cup toasted walnut oil

Combine all the ingredients and puree in a blender or food processor.

Roasted Veggie Salad

1 medium eggplant
2 red bell peppers
2 or 3 small zucchini
8 ounces mixed baby greens
2 tablespoons chopped fresh dill
2 tablespoons chopped fresh cilantro
1 cup cherry tomatoes
½ cup crumbled blue cheese or feta cheese
Olive oil for cooking
Garlic powder
Salt

Cut the eggplant into 3/8 inch thick slices. Brush both sides with olive oil. Lay the slices in a single layer on a baking sheet, sprinkle LIGHTLY with salt and broil on high on the top oven rack for 3-5 minutes till golden brown. Turn the slices and sprinkle lightly with garlic powder. Broil for 3-5 minutes until the second side is browned. Set aside on a plate to cool.

Seed and quarter the bell peppers and lay them out on the baking sheet. Slice the zucchini the long way, brush with olive oil and lay them on the baking sheet as well. Sprinkle the zucchini lightly with salt. Broil on high for 3-5 minutes on each side.

Mix the greens with the fresh herbs then put a fourth of the greens on each serving plate. Evenly distribute the roasted vegetables and tomatoes. Sprinkle with cheese and drizzle with balsamic vinaigrette just before serving.

Balsamic Vinaigrette

¼ cup Balsamic vinegar
½ cup olive oil
1 teaspoon Dijon mustard
Salt to taste

Combine the vinegar and mustard in a bowl and whisk until smooth.
Slowly add the oil as you continue to whisk.

Salt to taste.

For a special treat, use toasted walnut oil instead of olive oil.

Store extra for 3-4 days in a jar in the refrigerator.

Shake well before using.

Cucumber, Tomato & Avocado Salad

1 English cucumber peeled and diced
1 pint cherry tomatoes halved
1 large avocado diced
Garlic powder
¼ cup Italian dressing (page 63)

Toss the vegetables together, sprinkle with garlic powder and drizzle the dressing on top.

The combination of tastes and textures makes this one of my favorite salads!

Quinoa Salad

1 cup red quinoa
½ cup sweet onion - finely diced
2 tablespoons lemon zest
2-3 tablespoons freshly squeezed lemon juice
¼ cup olive oil
Garlic powder to taste
Salt to taste
1 large English cucumber peeled, seeded and diced
2 small zucchini - diced
1 red bell pepper – seeded and diced
One bunch of cilantro - chopped
¼ cup dried parsley crumbled
1 pint of cherry tomatoes

Cook the quinoa per package instructions. Combine all the ingredients except for the tomatoes in a large bowl and gently mix together. Adjust the amounts of lemon juice, salt, garlic, and olive oil to taste.

Refrigerate till you're ready to serve. Add the tomatoes just before serving.
Do not refrigerate tomatoes. They become mushy and mealy.

Keeps in the refrigerator for three to four days.

Black Bean Salad

1 can black beans drained and rinsed
1 orange
2 cups strawberries
½ cup finely diced sweet onion
1 head of cilantro
1 red bell pepper seeded and diced
1 teaspoon grated fresh ginger root
1 teaspoon orange zest
2 tablespoons olive oil
1/3 cup fresh orange juice
Salt to taste

Drain the beans and rinse under running water till the water runs clear.
Zest then peel and dice the orange.
Cut the strawberries into halves or quarters depending on the size.
Chop the cilantro leaves discarding any heavy stems.

Put the ginger, orange juice, orange zest and olive oil in a small bowl and whisk to combine. Combine the remaining ingredients in a large bowl. Drizzle the dressing over the top and toss gently. Salt to taste.

Serve as a side dish to chicken or fish or over mixed greens as a salad.

Mediterranean Chickpea Salad

1 can of Garbanzo beans drained and rinsed
¼ sweet onion finely diced (about 1/3 cup)
1 red bell pepper seeded and diced
1-2 teaspoons dill weed
2 tablespoons dried parsley
2 small zucchini thinly sliced
¼ cup Kalamata olives pitted and sliced
Zest of one lemon
2 tablespoons lemon juice
2 tablespoons olive oil
Salt to taste

Combine all the ingredients in a large bowl. Adjust the seasoning to taste. Serve over a bed of greens as a main dish or as a side to chicken or fish.

For an extra special salad, add some slices of grilled eggplant

Broccoli Slaw

1 pound broccoli slaw
2 carrots peeled and shredded
½ cup dried cherries
¾ cup roasted, salted cashews
¼ cup GF honey-mustard dressing
2 teaspoons horseradish
Salt to taste

Toss the broccoli, carrots, cherries and nuts together in a large bowl. Whisk together the dressing and horseradish then pour it over the veggie mixture and toss to distribute evenly.

Asian Pasta Salad

8 ounces gluten-free pasta shells
2 cups broccoli florets
1 cup sugar snap or snow peas
2 large oranges
1 head green onions
1 cup walnut halves

Cook the pasta al dente.
Steam the broccoli for 3-4 minutes.
Steam the snap peas for 1-2 minutes then immerse them in ice water.
Zest the oranges then peel, cut in half and then slice.
Thinly slice the onions- greens and whites.
Toss all the ingredients together in a large serving bowl.

Dressing

¼ cup gluten free tamari sauce
¼ cup honey
¼ cup toasted sesame oil
1 teaspoons grated fresh ginger root
2 teaspoons finely grated orange zest
¼ teaspoon garlic powder
A dash of cayenne
3 tablespoons orange juice
Optional: ¼ teaspoon red pepper flakes

Put the tamari sauce, ginger, garlic and cayenne in a microwave safe bowl. Allow the mixture to steep in the refrigerator for several hours or overnight.

Warm the mixture in a microwave or on the stove top in a small sauce pan then add the honey, oil and orange juice to taste. Pour the dressing over the veggies, pasta and nuts then toss to mix.

It's best if this salad can sit for at least 30 minutes before serving, but it's not very good after being refrigerated over night because the pasta gets mushy.

Serve at room temperature.

Optional: add either flaked grilled salmon or slices of grilled chicken breast.

Italian Pasta Salad

12 ounces GF fusilli cooked al dente
1 box frozen artichoke hearts
¼ sweet onion finely diced (½ cup)
1 red bell pepper seeded and diced
1 yellow bell pepper seeded and diced
1 cucumber seeded and diced
½ cup black olives sliced
2 tablespoons dried parsley
1 pint cherry tomatoes
½ cup freshly grated parmesan
Salt to taste
¼ - ½ cup Italian dressing (below)

Prepare the pasta and artichoke hearts according to package directions. Cool the pasta under running water. Toss all the ingredients except for the tomatoes and parmesan together with the dressing. Serve immediately or refrigerate for up to 2 hours. Toss in the tomatoes and parmesan just before serving.

Italian Dressing

¼ cup Balsamic vinegar
½ cup olive oil
1 teaspoon Dijon mustard
1 teaspoon dried basil
½ teaspoon garlic powder
Salt to taste

63

Soups

Cold Zucchini Soup

2 tablespoons butter
½ white onion diced (1 cup)
4 medium zucchini diced
4 cups chicken broth
½ cup plain yogurt
Salt and pepper to taste

Sauté the onions in the butter over medium-low heat until they are transparent. Add the zucchini and chicken broth. Bring to a boil then simmer for 15 minutes. Puree in a blender or food processor. Add the yogurt and whirl until combined. Season to taste.

Serve warm or chilled.

Garnish with a dollop of yogurt or sour cream.

Green Pea Soup

2 tablespoons butter
½ white onion diced (1 cup)
1 pound frozen peas
2½ cups water
½ teaspoon salt

Sauté the onions in the butter over medium-low heat until they are transparent. Add the salt and water then cover and bring to a boil over high heat. Add the peas and cook until they have just come back to a boil.

Puree in a blender or food processor till smooth. Serve immediately or chill and serve cold.

Garnish with mint leaves or cilantro leaves.

Carrot Soup

1 white onion diced
2 tablespoons corn oil
1 quart chicken or vegetable broth
1½ pounds carrots shredded
½ teaspoon salt

Sauté the onion in the oil until it is soft and translucent. Add the remaining ingredients and simmer for 8-10 minutes until the carrots are soft.

When I was seventeen, I worked as an Au Pair in Paris. My employer prepared this soup several times a week for her family. It soon became a main stay of my diet as well. Eating it still brings back happy memories!

Gazpacho

½ small sweet onion (about ½ cup)
3 or 4 cloves garlic
3 Serrano chilies (pith and seeds removed)
2 red bell peppers (pith and seeds removed)
1 English cucumber (peeled and seeded)
1 pound tomatoes (canned are OK)
2 slices GF sandwich bread*
2-3 ounces Olive Oil
1 teaspoon dry basil
2 teaspoon dry dill weed
½ teaspoon salt
1 teaspoon sugar
2 teaspoons Balsamic vinegar
1½ cups V-8 vegetable juice

Put the onion, garlic and chilies into food processor and pulse until very fine. Add the bell peppers and pulse till fine. Add the tomatoes and cucumber and pulse till coarsely chopped. Pour the mixture into a large serving bowl.

Put the bread into the food processor and process until it forms fine crumbs. With the processor still on, slowly add olive oil till the mixture forms a shiny paste. Add the remaining ingredients and blend thoroughly. Pour into the bowl of pureed vegetables and mix.

Chill at least 2 hours before serving.

Keeps 2-3 days in refrigerator but it's best the first day.

You may substitute ¾ cup Marcona almonds for the bread.

Serve with bowls of diced condiments such as cucumber, red bell pepper, zucchini, avocado, green onions and sour cream.

I always serve Poblano green jalapeno sauce on the side.

Roasted Tomato & Red Pepper Soup

2 pounds cherry tomatoes or Roma tomatoes
2 red bell peppers
½ cup sweet onion diced
½ teaspoon ground coriander powder
2-3 tablespoons olive oil
2 cups vegetable broth or chicken broth
Parmesan cheese to garnish

Optional: Add 2 tablespoons chopped fresh basil just before serving.

Cut the cherry tomatoes in half or quarter the Roma tomatoes and remove the seeds.
Seed the peppers and cut into one- inch pieces.
Lay all the veggies on a baking sheet, sprinkle with the coriander, a little salt and the olive oil. Toss with your hands to coat evenly.

Roast at 350° for 45 minutes stirring once half way through.

Warm the stock in a pan then add the roasted veggies. Puree with an emersion blender or in a regular blender.

Top with grated parmesan cheese.

Serves 4

Winter Squash Soup

2 tablespoons butter
½ white onion diced (1 cup)
1 butternut squash peeled and diced
4 cups chicken broth
½ teaspoon salt
½ teaspoon grated fresh ginger root
¼ teaspoon ground cumin
Fresh cilantro to garnish
Salt and pepper to taste

Sauté the onions in the butter over medium-low heat until they are transparent. Add the squash, ginger, cumin and chicken broth. Bring to a boil then simmer for **20-25 minutes** until the squash is tender. Puree with an emersion blender. Season to taste.

Garnish with a dollop of yogurt or sour cream and a few fresh cilantro leaves.

Black Bean Soup

1 pound black beans
½ large white onion (1 cup finely diced)
2 cloves garlic finely diced
2 tablespoons olive oil
1 teaspoon whole cumin seeds
1 teaspoon ground coriander powder
½ teaspoon ground cumin
A dash of cayenne
1 tablespoon New Mexico chili powder
1 teaspoon salt
2 bay leaves
1 ounce tomato paste
1 carrot peeled and diced

Wash and soak the black beans in the refrigerator for at least twelve hours then drain and rinse them before cooking.

Sauté the onions in the olive oil till they are soft and beginning to caramelize. Add the garlic and cumin seeds and sauté another minute. Do NOT brown the garlic, it will get bitter. Add the remaining ingredients plus enough water to go about 2 inches above the top of the beans (about six cups) and stir till the tomato paste is totally blended into the water.

Simmer 3-4 hours till the beans are soft.

Remove the bay leaves then purée with a hand blender. I don't make the soup totally smooth. I like it to still have bits of beans so that it has a rustic feel.

If the soup is too thick, add a little more water then bring it back to a simmer.

Drizzle a little Chipotle Cream on top of each bowl of soup just before serving.

Can be made ahead and re-heated.

Chipotle Cream

½ cup sour cream
½-1 teaspoon dried chipotle powder (to taste)
1 tablespoon water

Blend together until smooth.

Split Pea Shiitake Mushroom Soup

1½ pounds green split peas
2 tablespoons olive oil or corn oil
1 large onion diced (2 cups)
1½ pounds carrots peeled and cut into chunks
4 bay leaves
1-2 cups dried shiitake mushrooms crumbled
2 teaspoons GF bouillon
Salt to taste
2 quarts water

2 cups of frozen peas (thawed)

In a large pot, sauté the onions in the oil till lightly caramelized.

Wash and drain the split peas.

Add the peas and the remaining ingredients to the pot. Bring to a boil then cover and simmer until the peas are soft (about three hours). Add extra water if needed.

Remove the bay leaves then puree the soup with an emersion blender.

Stir in the green peas just before serving and heat until they are just warmed through.

Fifteen Bean Soup

2 tablespoons olive oil
2 onions diced
1 pound 15 bean mix
2-3 ounces mixed dried mushrooms
2 pounds carrots peeled and sliced
8 cups water or chicken broth
1 teaspoon salt
2 bay leaves
2 cups frozen peas

Rinse the beans then soak them over night in the refrigerator.

Sauté the onions in the olive oil over medium heat until they are caramelized. Drain and rinse the beans then add them to the pot with the carrots, water, salt and bay leaves. Crumble the mushrooms in your hands as you add them to the pot. Bring to a boil then cover and simmer for 3-4 hours until all the beans are soft. Add more water if needed.

Just before serving, remove the bay leaves and add the peas. Continue cooking until the peas are just warmed through.

Keeps for several days in the refrigerator.

Vegetable Soup with Pesto

2 tablespoons olive oil
2 onions diced
4 cloves garlic
4 ounces tomato paste
1 can of garbanzo beans
1 pound of red new potatoes quartered
8 cups water
1 teaspoon salt
2 teaspoons dried basil
Cayenne pepper to taste
1 pound green beans
1 pound frozen mixed vegetables (peas, carrots, corn and baby lima beans)
8 cups water or broth
1 bay leaf

Pesto (recipe follows)

Sauté the onions in the olive oil over medium heat until they are caramelized. Add the diced garlic and sauté for another minute then add the tomato paste and sauté stirring constantly until the past changes from out of the can red to orange.

Drain and rinse the garbanzo beans then add them along with the potatoes, water, salt, basil and bay leaves. Cover and simmer for 15 minutes then add the green beans and cook for 5 minutes then add the mixed vegetables and cook for another 5-10 minutes until they are tender.

Garnish each bowl of soup with a tablespoon of pesto.

Pesto

2 cloves garlic
2 cups basil leaves
½ cup grated parmesan cheese
½ cup olive oil

In a food processor:
Pulse the garlic till finely chopped then add the basil leaves and pulse till chopped. Add the cheese and pulse to mix. With the food processor turned on, slowly pour in the olive oil.

Creamy Corn Chowder

2 cups white onion finely diced (one large onion)
2 tablespoons butter
4½ cups half and half
½ cup water
1 teaspoon salt
10 cups fresh corn cut off the cob (about 10 ears)
1 teaspoon sugar

Sweat the onions in the butter till soft, but not brown. Add the remaining ingredients and bring to a simmer. Cook for 8 minutes. Do not let it come to a rolling boil or it may curdle. Remove the corn and puree in a blender till smooth then return it to the pot. Simmer for 2 more minutes to allow the natural corn starch to thicken the soup.

If you want to re-heat, use very low heat so it doesn't curdle.

If you're craving creamed corn, simply decrease the liquid by 1½ cups and only puree half the corn.

Chili Corn Chowder

1 cup white onion finely diced
1 tablespoon butter
3 cups half and half
½ cup water
½ teaspoon salt
5 cups fresh corn cut off the cob (about 6 ears)
1 cup diced, roasted mild New Mexico chilies
½ teaspoon ground cumin
A dash of cayenne
1 teaspoon GF chicken bouillon or 2 packs Trader Joe's reduced sodium chicken broth concentrate
Optional: 1½ cups diced cooked chicken

Sweat the onions in the butter till they are soft, but not brown. Add the remaining ingredients (except for the chicken) and bring to simmer. Cook for 8 minutes. Do not let it come to a rolling boil or the cream may curdle. Puree with a hand blender. (If you are going to add chicken, add it now.) Simmer for two or three minutes to allow the natural corn starch to thicken the soup.

Garnish with shredded sharp cheddar cheese.

Best fresh. If you must re-heat, use very low heat so it doesn't curdle or microwave at 30% power till it's warm. **Do not allow the soup to come to a boil.**

Broccoli Cheddar Soup

½ **white onion** diced
2 tablespoons butter
¼ **cup Better Batter GF flour**
2 cups chicken broth
2 cups whole milk or half and half
1 pound chopped broccoli
1 cup extra sharp cheddar cheese

Steam the broccoli till it's tender.

Sauté the onion in the butter until it is soft and translucent. Sprinkle the Better Batter over the onions and cook for a minute then slowly pour in the chicken stock whisking constantly to prevent lumps. Simmer for several minutes stirring constantly until it thickens. Whisk in the milk and add broccoli and simmer for several minutes until warm. Puree with an emersion blender. Fold in the cheese just before serving.

Garnish with steamed broccoli florets.

Serves 4

Coconut Corn Crab Chowder

2 cups white onion finely diced
2 tablespoons butter
4 cups coconut milk
1 cup water or chicken broth
5 cups fresh corn cut off the cob (about 5 ears)
½ cup mild green chilies*
1 teaspoon salt
1 teaspoon grated ginger root
¼ teaspoon ground cumin
1 teaspoon sugar
1 pound of lump crab meat**
Optional: 1 tablespoon fresh Thai basil chopped

Sweat the onions in the butter till soft, but not brown. Add the remaining ingredients except for the crab and bring to a simmer. Cook for 8 minutes. Remove the corn and puree in a blender till smooth then return it to the pot. Simmer for 2 more minutes to allow the natural corn starch to thicken the soup. Fold in the crab meat just before serving and warm for a minute or two.

Serve fresh.

*I prefer frozen chopped Hatch chilies, but canned green chilies will work too.

** If fresh crab is not available, either frozen or pasteurized refrigerated crab meat are both quite good. Diced cooked chicken will also work well in this recipe.

Main Dishes

Spinach and Feta Quiche

1 medium yellow onion diced
1 tablespoon olive oil
1 teaspoon dried dill weed
2 cups chopped spinach thawed and drained
¼ cup sundried tomatoes drained and diced
6 ounces feta cheese crumbled
4 eggs
1 cup milk
¼ teaspoon salt
A dash of cayenne

Cream cheese crust (recipe follows)

Sauté the onion in the olive oil until it begins to caramelize. Add the dill and cook for a few seconds then remove from heat and mix with the spinach and sun dried tomatoes. Gently fold in the cheese then spread the filling in the bottom of a partially cooked crust.

Whisk the eggs, milk, salt and pepper together in a large bowl then slowly pour over the vegetable and cheese mixture. Gently nudge the filling with a spoon so the eggs distribute evenly.

Bake at 350° for 45-55 minutes
To test for doneness, gently nudge the pan. If the center still jiggles, it's not done yet

Allow to cool for at least five minutes before slicing.

Cream Cheese Crust

1/3 cup butter
2 ounces cream cheese
¼ teaspoon salt
½ teaspoon sugar
½ cup + 2 tablespoons Better Batter GF flour
½ cup + 3 tablespoons blanched almond flour
3 tablespoons cold water
Extra almond flour for rolling out dough

Place the dry ingredients in a food processor and pulse until well mixed. Dice the COLD butter and cream cheese and add to the food processor. Pulse until the dough looks like peas. Add the water and pulse.

Turn the dough into a bowl and kneed once or twice till the dough just comes together. Wrap the dough in plastic wrap and refrigerate it for at least two hours or overnight.

Lay the dough on a sheet of parchment paper that has been sprinkled with almond flour. Sprinkle more almond flour on top before you cover it with a second sheet of parchment. Roll the dough between the two pieces of parchment paper till it's about 2 inches larger in diameter than your pie tin.

Turn the dough into a nonstick 9 inch pie tin. Gently fit it into the pan and crimp the top to make it pretty. Pierce the bottom multiple times with a fork so that air pockets won't form when you bake it.

If you're it in a recipe that requires further baking:
Pre-bake the crust for ten minutes at 350°

If you are going to add a filling that does not need further baking:
Bake at 350° for 12-15 minutes, till it's golden brown.

Asparagus Quiche

4 eggs
1 cup whole milk
½ teaspoon salt
A dash of cayenne
1 cup raw asparagus thinly sliced
6 asparagus spears to decorate the top
½ cup green onions thinly sliced whites and greens
1 cup shredded sharp cheddar cheese

Butter crust (recipe follows)

Whisk the eggs, milk, salt and pepper together in a large bowl.

In a separate bowl gently mix the asparagus, onions and cheese then put them in the partially baked crust.

Slowly pour the egg mixture over the veggies and cheese. Gently nudge the veggies with a spoon so the eggs distribute evenly.

Bake at 350° for 45-55 minutes
To test for doneness, gently nudge the pan. If the center still jiggles, it's not done yet.

Allow to cool for several minutes before slicing.

Butter Crust

6 tablespoons very cold butter
½ cup Better Batter GF flour
½ cup blanched almond flour
¼ teaspoon salt
½ teaspoon sugar
3 tablespoons cold water
Extra almond flour to roll out the dough

Combine all the dry ingredients in a food processor and pulse till well blended. Cut the butter into half inch cubes. Toss the butter into the food processor and pulse until the mixture forms pea sized bits. Add the water and pulse till the dough just begins to come together. Turn the dough into a bowl, knead once or twice then form a ball. Wrap the dough in plastic wrap and refrigerate for at least one hour (up to two days).

Roll the dough between two pieces of parchment or wax paper that have been generously dusted with almond flour. Roll until it is 2 inches larger in diameter than your pie pan. Use the paper to help transfer the dough to your pie pan. Pierce the dough multiple times with a fork prior to baking.

Bake at 350° for 10 minutes if you are going to use the crust for a recipe that requires further cooking.

Bake for 12-15 minutes until golden brown if the recipe requires no further cooking.

Mushroom Quiche

1 medium yellow onion diced
1 tablespoon olive oil
¼ teaspoon dried rosemary
12 ounces fresh cremini mushrooms sliced
3 ounces cheddar cheese grated
3 ounces gruyere cheese grated
4 eggs
1 cup milk
¼ teaspoon salt
A dash of cayenne

1 recipe cream cheese crust (page 85)

Sauté the onion in the olive oil until it begins to caramelize. Add the mushrooms and rosemary and sauté till they begin to brown and the excess water is absorbed. Gently mix in the cheese then spread the filling in the bottom of a partially cooked crust.

Whisk the eggs, milk, salt and pepper together in a large bowl then slowly pour over the vegetable and cheese mixture. Gently nudge the filling with a spoon so the eggs distribute evenly.

Bake at 350° for 45-55 minutes

To test for doneness, gently nudge the pan. If the center still jiggles, it's not done yet

Allow to cool for at least five minutes before slicing.

Chili and Green Onion Quiche

4 eggs
1 cup milk
1 teaspoon California chili powder
¼ - ½ teaspoon salt
A dash of garlic powder
A dash of cayenne
1 cup diced roasted chilies thoroughly drained
½ cup green onions finely sliced
1 cup shredded sharp cheddar cheese

1 recipe cream cheese crust (page 85)

Whisk the eggs, milk, chili powder, salt, pepper and garlic together in a large bowl.

In a separate bowl gently mix the chilies, onions and cheese then place them into a partially cooked crust (see cream cheese crust recipe).

Slowly pour the egg mixture over the filling. Gently nudge the filling with a spoon so the eggs distribute evenly.

Bake at 350° for 45-55 minutes
To test for doneness, gently nudge the pan. If the center still jiggles, it's not done yet
Allow to cool for a couple minutes before slicing

Chiles Rellenos Casserole

10 Hatch chilies
6 eggs
2 tablespoons Better Batter GF flour
1½ cups whole milk
½ teaspoon salt
1 teaspoon California chili powder
1/8 teaspoon garlic powder
A dash of cayenne
¼ cup dried chives
6 ounces pepper jack cheese grated
6 ounces extra sharp cheddar cheese grated
1 pat of butter for the pan

Broil the chilies on high for 3-5 minutes on each side till they are blistered and brown then put them in a paper bag for about 10 minutes. Peel and seed the chilies and set them aside. This can be done in advance and the chilies can be refrigerated for several days or frozen for months.

Beat the eggs with an electric mixer then add the flour and beat until completely blended. Add the milk, salt, chili powder and garlic powder and chives and mix.

Generously butter the bottom and sides of a 7 by 9 inch baking dish.

Pour a little of the egg mixture in the baking dish. Open the chilies and lay half of them on the bottom of the dish. It's OK if they overlap a little. Mix the two cheeses together then sprinkle half the cheese over the chilies. Top with a second layer of chilies. Sprinkle the rest of the cheese on top then pour the remaining egg mixture over the cheese. Gently nudge the cheese with a spoon so the egg mixture gets evenly distributed.

Bake at 350° for 40-50 minutes until the center is set.

Allow to cool for a few minutes before cutting.

Serves 6-8

Ricotta Stuffed Peppers

4 Anaheim peppers or 6 mild Hatch Chilies
8 ounces ricotta cheese
3 tablespoons grated Parmesan
3 tablespoons grated Romano cheese
1 egg
1½ cups tomato sauce (recipe follows)
Extra parmesan to sprinkle on top

Place the peppers under the broiler till they blister (3-5 minutes on each side) then put them in a sealed paper bag for about 10 minutes. Peel the peppers then slit them down one side to remove the seeds. Keep the peppers whole.

Combine all the cheeses. Mix in the egg. Fill the peppers with the cheese mixture and place on a baking sheet.

Pour sauce over the peppers. Sprinkle with parmesan cheese.

Bake at 350° for 45 minutes.

Optional: add 1 cup chopped spinach that has been thawed and drained to the ricotta combo.

Serve as a main dish with a salad; or serve with pasta.

Tomato Sauce

2 sweet onions diced
2 tablespoons olive oil
6-8 cloves garlic finely minced
2 teaspoons fennel seeds
1 teaspoon red chili flakes
2 tablespoons dried sweet basil
1 teaspoon sugar
2 red bell peppers
30 ounces tomato PASTE
45 ounces water
Salt to taste

Sauté the onions in the olive oil till they are caramelize. Add the garlic, fennel and chili flakes and sauté another minute. Add the tomato past and stir constantly until the color changes from "out of the can red" to orange. Add the water a little at a time stirring till well blended. Add the diced red bell peppers. Crush the basil between your hands to release the oils as you add it to the pot.

Simmer for at least 20 minutes.

Puree with a hand blender.

This sauce will keep for several days in the refrigerator. Freezes well.

I freeze single serving amounts of leftover sauce in zip lock bags.

Ratatouille Casserole

1½ cups onion diced
½ head garlic diced
2 tablespoons olive oil
2-3 teaspoons crushed red pepper
3 teaspoons fennel seeds
1 teaspoon sugar
2 tablespoons dried basil
Garlic powder
Salt to taste
1¼ pound 85/15 ground turkey
2 cans of chickpeas drained and rinsed
2 cans petite diced tomatoes
6-8 small Zucchini coarsely cubed
3 red, yellow or orange bell peppers seeded and coarsely diced
½ large egg plant diced (do not peel)
1/3 cup uncooked rice (If you use brown rice, par boil it for about 15 minutes.)

Sauté the onions in olive oil till they begin to caramelize then add the garlic and one teaspoon chili flakes then cook for another couple minutes. Push the onions mixture to the side of the pan drop in the ground turkey, break it up and sprinkle it with the fennel seeds, remaining chili, salt, garlic powder and sugar. Sauté till the meat is brown.

(You're turning the turkey into sweet Italian sausage.)

Add all the remaining ingredients. Sprinkle with salt and garlic powder to taste. Mix well then turn into a jelly roll pan.

Bake covered at 350° for 30 minutes.

Stir and return to the oven uncovered for another 30-40 minutes.

Sprinkle with parmesan cheese before serving.

Oven "Fried" Chicken

1 whole chicken cut up
2 cups gluten-free corn flakes
1½ teaspoons garlic powder
1 teaspoon sugar
¼ teaspoon salt
1 tablespoon corn oil

Whirl the cornflakes in a food processor to form fine crumbs. Put the cornflake crumbs, garlic, sugar and salt in a plastic bag and shake until well mixed. Add the oil and massage the bag of seasoned crumbs until the oil is totally distributed.

Put the chicken in the bag one piece at a time and shake to coat. Lay the coated pieces of chicken on a baking sheet. Space the chicken out enough so the pieces don't touch each other.

Bake at 350° for 45-55 minutes.

Chicken Pot Pie

1 pound fresh mushrooms - sliced
2 tablespoons butter
2 teaspoons oil
A pinch of rosemary
A pinch of thyme
2 cups frozen mixed veggies (peas, carrots, green beans)
1 cup frozen peas
½ cup frozen pearl onions
3 cups cooked chicken diced
1 quart chicken broth
1 teaspoon GF chicken bouillon
1 cup half and half or whole milk
¼ cup Better Batter GF flour
2 tablespoons butter

Cream cheese crust (page 85)

For the filling:
Sauté the mushrooms, rosemary and thyme in 2 tablespoons butter plus 2 teaspoons oil.

Melt 2 tablespoons butter in a three quart sauce pan over medium-low heat. Then sprinkle in the Better Batter and sauté for a minute. Gradually whisk in the chicken broth. Continue whisking till smooth. Bring to a simmer. Add the chicken and veggies and simmer till everything is warm. Add the cream and cook till the mixture reaches a simmer.

For the crust:
Prepare the dough for the pie crust and refrigerate it for at least an hour or up to two days. Roll out the crust and cut it into circles that are slightly smaller in diameter than the bowls you plan to use as individual serving dishes.

Place the dough circles on a non-stick or parchment paper lined baking sheet. Pierce each circle multiple times with a fork.

Bake at 350° for 12-15 minutes till golden brown.

Ladle the chicken and vegetable stew into individual serving bowls or mugs and top each with a circle of cooked crust immediately before serving.

Serves 4-6

Vegetable Curry

2 onions
2 tablespoons light oil
3 cloves garlic minced
1 tablespoon fresh grated ginger root
½ teaspoon turmeric
1 teaspoon whole cumin seeds
½ teaspoon coriander powder
½ teaspoon crushed red chili
Cayenne pepper to taste
Salt to taste
1 head of cauliflower
1 can petite diced tomatoes
1 red bell pepper seeded and sliced
1 can garbanzo beans drained and rinsed
2 cups green beans cut into thirds
¾ cups plain yogurt

Peel the onions, cut them in half lengthwise then slice thinly. Sauté the onion in the oil until it begins to caramelize. Add the remaining spices and cook for a minute until the aromas come out and the seeds begin to pop. Add the cauliflower, tomatoes and garbanzo beans cover and cook until the cauliflower is soft (about 15 minutes). Add the bell pepper and green beans, cover then cook another 6 to 8 minutes. Fold in the yogurt just before serving.

Serve over steamed basmati rice or with roasted potatoes.

Serves 4.

Quick Chicken Curry

1 onion
2 tablespoons light oil
2 cloves garlic minced
1 tablespoon fresh grated ginger root
½ teaspoon turmeric
½ teaspoon whole cumin seeds
½ teaspoon coriander powder
½ teaspoon crushed red chili
Cayenne pepper to taste
Salt to taste
1 pound boneless, skinless chicken thinly sliced
1 large tomato seeded and diced
1 red bell pepper seeded and sliced
1 jalapeno pepper seeded and sliced
1 apple peeled and diced
½ cup plain yogurt

Peel the onion, cut it in half the long way then slice thinly. Sauté the onion in the oil until it begins to caramelize. Add the remaining spices and cook for a minute until the aromas come out and the seeds begin to pop. Add the chicken and sauté 1-2 minutes. Add the tomato, peppers, and apple then cook until the chicken is done about 4-5 minutes till the chicken is cooked through. Fold in the yogurt just before serving.

Serve over steamed basmati rice or with roasted potatoes.

Serves 4

Pasta with Spinach, Mushrooms and Sun-Dried Tomatoes

12 ounces GF pasta spirals or butterflies
12 ounces cremini mushroom - sliced
4 garlic cloves - finely diced
3 tablespoons butter
8 ounce jar sun-dried tomatoes
8 ounces fresh baby spinach
Salt to taste
½ cup pine nuts
Several fresh basil leaves - julienned
6 ounces feta cheese or fresh goat cheese

Cook the pasta per package directions.

In the meantime:
Sauté the nuts over low heat in a dry pan till they just begin to brown then put them on a plate.

Sauté the garlic in the butter mixed with a little of the oil from the sun dried tomatoes for a minute. (Do NOT brown the garlic or it will be bitter.) Add the mushrooms and sauté until they are brown and the liquid is absorbed. Salt to taste.

Drain the sun dried tomatoes and add them to the pan. Sauté until the tomatoes begin to caramelize. Add the spinach and sauté for a minute until the spinach is warm and just wilted. Fold in the cooked pasta and sauté for a minute. Remove from heat, fold in the basil and crumbled feta or goat cheese.

Turn onto a serving platter and sprinkle with the toasted pine nuts.

Serves 4

Variations:
Substitute toasted walnut halves for the pine nuts.
For extra flavor, protein and fiber use buckwheat pasta.

This dish has long been one of my favorite company dinners. It's easy, delicious and so pretty it looks like it came from a fine restaurant.

Fettuccini with Broccoli

1 pound GF fettuccini
1 pound chopped broccoli
1 onion diced
2 tablespoons olive oil or butter
8 ounces fresh cremini mushrooms
1½ cups sour cream
½ cup grated parmesan cheese

Cook the pasta till al dente.

Lightly steam the broccoli.

Sauté the onion in the olive oil till it begins to brown. Add the sliced mushrooms and sauté until they are cooked and any excess liquid has evaporated. Fold in all the remaining ingredients and heat until warm.

Serve with extra parmesan cheese on the side.

This recipe also works well with chopped spinach instead of broccoli.

Turkey Tetrazzini

¾ pound brown rice pasta shells or fusilli
1 pound fresh mushrooms sliced
1 stick butter
1 teaspoon oil
3 cups diced cooked turkey (or chicken)
¼ teaspoon dried rosemary finely crushed
¼ teaspoon garlic powder
Salt to taste
5 packets of Trader Joe's concentrated reduced
   sodium chicken broth or 2 teaspoons other GF
   chicken bouillon
¼ cup Better Batter GF flour
3 cups whole milk
¼ cup water
1 cup coarsely chopped pecans
Butter for the pan

Cook the pasta for **half** the recommended cooking time. Then drain and rinse with cold water.

Sauté the mushrooms, garlic and rosemary in 2 tablespoons of butter plus one teaspoon of oil. Salt at the end of cooking.

In a large sauce pan, melt ½ stick of butter. Sprinkle the Better Batter over the butter and sauté for a minute then slowly whisk in the water and milk. Continue whisking until the mixture is smooth. Add the bouillon and simmer until the mixture thickens. Taste the sauce and salt to taste. Fold in the mushrooms and pasta then turn into a buttered 13 by 9 inch nonstick pan.

Sprinkle the pecans over the top and then dot with the remaining butter.

Bake at 350° for 45 minutes

Serves 8

Turkey tetrazzini has always been one of my favorite after-Thanksgiving comfort foods. Coming up with a satisfying gluten-free version made me a very happy camper last winter!

Lasagna

8 GF lasagna noodles
4½ cups tomato sauce (page 94)
1 pound ricotta cheese
¼ teaspoon salt
2 eggs
1 pound mozzarella cheese grated
½ cup grated parmesan
¼ cup grated Romano cheese

Cook the pasta for **one minute less than HALF** the recommended cooking time then drain.

In a large bowl mix the ricotta, eggs and salt until smooth. Fold in ¾ of the mozzarella cheese and all the parmesan and Romano. Set aside the rest of the mozzarella cheese.

In a 9 inch loaf pan:
Spread 1½ cups of sauce in the bottom of the pan.
Top with 2 noodles.
Spread half the cheese mixture over the top.
Top with 2 more noodles.
Spread 1½ cups sauce over the noodles.
Top with 2 more noodles.
Spread the rest of the cheese mixture on top.
Top with 2 more noodles.
Spread the rest of the sauce on top.

Place the pan on a baking sheet to catch any spills.

Bake at 350° for 45 minutes

Remove from the oven and top with the remaining mozzarella cheese.

Bake for another 15-20 minutes till the cheese is melted and golden brown.

Serves 6

I have always preferred vegetarian lasagna, but if you simply must have meat I suggest that you sauté a pound of your favorite ground meat or sausage with an onion and some garlic and a tablespoon of fennel seeds, then mix it with 2 cups of tomato sauce. Just ladle some meat sauce over each slice of lasagna as you serve it.

Roasted Eggplant Parmesan

1 medium eggplant
¼ cup olive oil
Salt
Garlic powder
2 cups tomato sauce (page 94)
1½ cups shredded mozzarella cheese
¼ cup grated parmesan cheese

8 slices of polenta (recipe follows)

Cut the eggplant into eight slices. Do *not* remove the skin. Brush each side with olive oil and lay on a baking sheet. Sprinkle the top with salt then broil on high for 5-7 minutes, until the eggplant is golden brown. Turn the slices over, sprinkle with a little garlic powder then broil the second side for another 4-6 minutes until brown.

In the meantime, warm the sauce and sauté the sliced polenta.

To assemble: Put a little sauce on top of each slice of polenta. Top with a slice of eggplant and a little more sauce, a handful of mozzarella and a sprinkle of parmesan.

Place under the broiler on a low rack for 1-2 minutes until the cheese is melted and beginning to brown.

Serve with a salad or steamed vegetables.

Polenta

4 cups water
1 tablespoon butter
¼ teaspoon salt
1¼ cups yellow corn meal
1 cup grated parmesan cheese
¼ cup grated Romano cheese

Put the water, butter and salt in a 3 quart sauce pan. Heat over high heat until it comes to a boil. Slowly add the corn meal, a little at a time while whisking constantly to prevent lumps from forming. Cook over low heat stirring constantly with a pancake turner until the mixture is extremely thick, **about 20 minutes.**
Then stir in the cheese.

Pour into an 8½ inch loaf pan that has been lined with plastic wrap. Cover with plastic wrap. Allow the polenta to cool to room temperature then refrigerate for at least 6 hours.

To serve, remove the polenta from the loaf pan and cut into half inch thick slices. Sauté in olive oil over medium heat until it's golden and crisp on both sides.

For extra crisp polenta: Before you sauté, dip the large sides in potato starch, brush off any excess then sauté in olive oil as usual.

Side Dishes

Wild Rice Pilaf

1 cup wild rice
1 onion diced
2 tablespoons olive oil
8 ounces fresh cremini mushrooms
1 ounce mixed dried mushrooms
2¼ cups water or chicken broth
¼ teaspoon salt
¼ teaspoon dried thyme
¼ teaspoon dried rosemary

Wash the rice under running water then soak it for at least an hour, drain and rinse again.

Sauté the onion in the olive oil till it begins to caramelize. Slice the fresh mushrooms and add them to the pan. Sauté until they are brown. Crumble the dried mushrooms on top then add all the remaining ingredients.

Cover and simmer for 45 minutes or until the rice is tender. Add a little more broth if needed.

Sweet and Savory Rice

1 onion diced
2 tablespoons butter
½ teaspoon whole cumin seeds
¼ teaspoon ground coriander
A dash of cayenne pepper
1 cup basmati rice
½ cup diced red bell pepper diced
½ cup diced dried apricots
¼ cup dried currants
¼ teaspoon salt
2 cups chicken or vegetable broth

Sauté the onion in the butter until it becomes translucent. Add the cumin and coriander and cook for about 30 seconds until the spices become fragrant. Stir in the rice and sauté for another minute then add all the remaining ingredients. Bring to a boil then cover and cook over low heat until the water is absorbed and the rice is tender.

Kasha
(Toasted Buckwheat Groat Pilaf)

1 small sweet onion finely diced
1 tablespoon corn oil (or other bland oil)
1 cup whole grain Kasha
1 egg
¼ teaspoon salt
1 teaspoon GF chicken bouillon
½ cup mixed dried mushrooms crumbled
8 ounces fresh cremini mushrooms sliced
3 cups water
Butter for garnish (optional)

Sauté the onion in the oil till lightly golden. Add the kasha and stir over medium heat until it starts to smell a bit toasty. (1-2 minutes) Beat the egg, add it to the pan. Stir quickly so that it coats the Kasha. Immediately add the remaining ingredients and bring to a boil.

Cover and simmer for 15-20 minutes till the water is absorbed and the grain is tender.

Serve with a pat of butter on top for extra richness.

To reheat leftovers, add a teaspoon of water, cover and microwave till warm.

Roasted Potatoes

1½ pounds small red potatoes
2 tablespoons olive oil
1 tablespoon butter melted
½ teaspoon garlic powder
1 teaspoon whole cumin seeds
¼ teaspoon crushed red pepper

Cut the potatoes in half. Add the remaining ingredients and toss to coat. Spread cut side down on a baking sheet.

Bake at 450° for 20-30 minutes till the potatoes are soft and golden brown.

Roasted Brussels Sprouts

1 pound of Brussels sprouts
2 tablespoons olive oil
Salt to taste

Trim the ends of the Brussels sprouts and cut them in half the long way. Place them on a cookie sheet, sprinkle with salt and the olive oil. Toss to coat. Lay the veggies cut side down.

Bake at 450° for 15-20 minutes till they just begin to brown.

Cabbage Sauté

½ sweet onion (about 1 cup)
1 head of cabbage
2 tablespoons olive oil
1 tablespoon butter
1 teaspoon dried dill weed
Salt to taste

Peel and thinly slice the onion. Core the cabbage and cut it into half-inch strips. Sauté the onion in the butter and olive oil till it's soft and beginning to caramelize. Add the cabbage and dill and continue to sauté until the cabbage is soft. Salt to taste.

Mixed Vegetable Sauté

1 onion
2 tablespoons olive oil
2 cloves garlic minced
1 pound cremini mushrooms sliced
1 red bell pepper seeded and sliced
½ pound yellow squash sliced
½ pound zucchini sliced
½ teaspoon dried basil
Salt and pepper to taste

Grated parmesan cheese

Peel the onion and cut it in half the long way then cut into thin slices. Sauté the onion in the olive oil till it begins to caramelize. Add the garlic and cook for another minute then add the sliced mushrooms and sauté until they begin to brown and any liquid is absorbed. Add the remaining vegetables, basil, salt and pepper. Cover for 2-3 minutes then remove the cover and continue to sauté until done.

Sprinkle with a little parmesan cheese just before serving.

Shiitake Lentils

1 pound lentils
1 cup diced sweet onion
1 clove garlic
2 tablespoons olive oil
1 ounce dried shiitake mushrooms
8 ounces fresh cremini mushrooms
1 teaspoon GF chicken bouillon
1 sweet potato
6 cups of water
Salt to taste

Sauté the onions in the olive oil until they begin they caramelize. Add the garlic and cook for another minute.

Grind the dried mushrooms into a fine powder in a coffee grinder or blender.
Wash the lentils.
Slice the mushrooms.
Peel and dice the sweet potato.

Add all the remaining ingredients into the pot with the garlic and onions. Bring to a boil then cover and simmer for 25-40 minutes until the water is absorbed and the lentils are soft. If necessary, add a little extra water.

Caribbean Sweet Potatoes

2 pounds sweet potatoes - peeled and sliced
2 pounds bananas - peeled and sliced
1 cup pecan pieces
½ stick butter
¼ cup dark rum
1 cup brown sugar
½ teaspoon salt

Layer the potatoes and bananas in a deep baking dish. Dot with butter. Combine the rum, sugar and salt then pour the mixture over the potatoes and bananas.

Bake covered at 375° for 40-45 minutes.

Remove from oven and top with the nuts and remaining butter. Baste the nuts with the sauce.

Return to oven uncovered for 10-15 minutes until the nuts are brown.

Topping alternative: Combine 1/3 cup each brown sugar, Better Batter GF flour, butter, shredded coconut and pecans.

Spread the topping over the cooked potatoes then return to the oven for 15-20 minutes, till the topping is brown.

Crepes
Savory and Sweet

Basic Crepes

5 extra-large eggs
½ cup Better Batter GF flour
¼ cup blanched almond flour
¼ teaspoon salt
2 teaspoons sugar
2 cups whole milk

Butter for the pan

Whisk the eggs and the dry ingredients till smooth, then slowly whisk in the milk till the batter is completely smooth. Refrigerate for at least 10 minutes then whisk again before cooking.

Warm an eight inch nonstick pan on medium heat then add a sliver of butter and turn to coat. When the butter is warm enough to sizzle add about ¼ cup of batter and slowly swirl the pan till it's coated. Pour excess batter back into the bowl. Cook for about 90 seconds till you can just barely see brown from the bottom and the top appears dry. Turn the crepe and cook for another 20-30 seconds till LIGHTLY browned.*

Turn the crepes onto a dish (they can be in a pile) until they are all prepared then either create your desert crepes or roll blintzes

Makes 20 eight inch crepes

*These crepes are rather fragile so you may find it easier to turn each crepe into a second buttered pan to cook the second side.

If you want to do a half recipe, use 2 eggs and start with only ¾ cups of milk.

Make a test "mini" crepe. If it's too thick, add a bit more milk

Cheese Blintzes

2 pounds ricotta cheese
2 eggs
1 tablespoon sugar
¼ teaspoon salt
Butter for the pan

1 recipe basic crepes (page 122)

Mix the ricotta, eggs, sugar and salt together in a large bowl.

Begin preparing the crepes. As each crepe is cooked, lay it on a work surface. Put 2 tablespoons of cheese mixture about a third of the way from one edge of the crepe. Fold in that edge and the two short edges then roll the crepe around the cheese (like a burrito). Set the blintzes on a plate as you make them. At this point they can be wrapped in plastic and refrigerated or frozen, or you can sauté and serve them right away.

To finish cooking: Melt a little butter in a large nonstick pan over medium-low heat. Place the blintzes about a half inch apart in the pan and sauté till they are golden brown, about 4-5 minutes per side.

Serve with sour cream.

Also good with warm fruit compote or cherry pie filling.

Lemony Dessert Crepes

One recipe basic crepes (page 122)
3 or 4 lemons
¼ cup sugar

Zest 3 lemons and set the zest aside.
Juice the lemons and strain out the seeds.
(If you run out of juice during preparation, use the fourth lemon.)

Lay three crepes on each plate. Sprinkle the crepes with a **little** sugar and then drizzle about a teaspoon of lemon juice on each one. Fold the crepes into fourths and lay them out so they overlap slightly. Top with a little more sugar, lemon juice and a pinch of lemon zest.

Serves 6

These crepes are extremely light and delicate, almost translucent. With a little practice, they come out perfectly, but if they are slightly imperfect, roll them into loose tubes instead of folding them. It will hide any little imperfections.

Crepes with Banana and Chocolate Sauce

1 recipe basic crepes (page 122)

For the filling:
6 bananas sliced
½ cup brown sugar
3 tablespoons butter
1 tablespoon dark rum

Melt the butter in a large nonstick pan over medium low heat. Add the sugar and bananas and sauté until the bananas are soft (6-8 minutes). Add the rum and continue to sauté for a couple minutes so the alcohol cooks out.

For the chocolate sauce:
1 cup of 60% chocolate chips
1 cup of heavy cream
½ teaspoon instant coffee granules
A pinch of salt

Combine the ingredients in the top of a double boiler and cook over low heat, stirring constantly until the chocolate is melted. Serve promptly.

To assemble: Put 2 tablespoons of filling on each the crepe then roll the crepe to form a tube. Place 3 crepes on each plate and drizzle with warm chocolate sauce.

Serves 6

Berries and Cream Crepes

One recipe basic crepes (page 122)

8 ounces mascarpone
4 ounces heavy cream
2 Tablespoons sugar

4 cups of fresh strawberries sliced
1 cup fresh raspberries
¼ cup sugar
2 Tablespoons Grand Marnier or Chambord raspberry liqueur

Fresh whole berries to decorate
Sweetened whipped cream (optional)

Prepare the berries in a large bowl, cover and allow to macerate in the refrigerator for at least 4 hours. Taste for sweetness and add a bit more sugar if needed.

Whip the mascarpone, cream and sugar together until light and fluffy.

Just before serving, prepare the crepes.
Put about 2 tablespoons of the cream mixture on each crepe and gently roll.
Put the filled crepes on serving plates 2 or 3 per serving.
Top with about 1/3 cup of macerated berries.

Decorate the plates with a few fresh berries and a dollop of whipped cream.

Biscuits and Cornbread

Spoon Biscuits

3 tablespoons frozen butter cut into small cubes
½ cup Better Batter GF flour
½ cup blanched almond flour
¼ teaspoon salt
½ teaspoon sugar
2 teaspoons baking powder
½ cup Fage 2% Greek yogurt
¼ cup whole milk

Optional: 1 teaspoon dried scallions + 1 teaspoon dried dill weed

After dicing the butter, put it into the freezer while you gather the rest of the ingredients.

Put all the dry ingredients into a food processor and pulse to mix. Add the butter and pulse till crumbly with pea size bits of butter still visible. Add the yogurt and milk then pulse till it just forms chunks of dough.

Drop the dough onto a plate. **Do not knead the dough. Do not touch the dough with your hands!** Use 2 spoons to gently divide the dough into 8 or 9 lumps and, still using the spoons, gently set them on a parchment paper lined baking sheet.

Bake at 425° for 15-18 minutes

Serve promptly.
If you need to re-heat leftovers, use a toaster oven. They don't do well in the microwave.

*In one of my favorite books, **The Crossroads Café** by **Deborah Smith**, the main character tries repeatedly to make biscuits using her down-home southern cousin's time-proven recipe. After many failures, she realizes that the secret ingredient is joy. Finally, her biscuits come out perfectly!*

After struggling to get my own biscuit recipe just right for weeks, it became a job instead of a joy, and the biscuits were getting worse with each try. Finally, after having a wonderful success with another recipe, I was in my "joy of baking mode" and quickly decided what changes needed to make to my biscuit recipe. I threw them together without allowing myself time to think.

At last, perfect biscuits! They're moist and buttery on the inside with a crunchy crust.

Enjoy!

Cheddar Biscuits

1 tablespoon butter
2 ounces extra sharp cheddar cheese
½ cup blanched almond flour
½ cup Better Batter GF flour
¼ teaspoon salt
¼ teaspoon sugar
2 teaspoons baking powder
A scant ¼ teaspoon garlic powder
A dash of cayenne pepper
1 teaspoon dried chives
½ cup Fage 2% Greek yogurt
3 Tablespoons whole milk

Dice the cheese and butter into small cubes and place in the freezer while you gather the rest of the ingredients.

Put the dry ingredients in a food processor and pulse to mix. Add the butter and cheese then pulse till the mixture is crumbly and you still see pea sized pieces of cheese. Add the yogurt and milk then pulse 2 or 3 times. The mixture should look like a lot of little wet blobs of dough that are only partially stuck together.

Turn the mixture onto a plate. **Do not touch the dough with your hands. Do not knead the dough or push it tightly together.** Using two spoons, gently separate the dough into 8 mounds and set them on a parchment lined baking sheet.

Bake at 425° for 15-18 minutes

Serve warm.

If you need to re-heat use a toaster oven. They don't do well in the microwave.

Before I had to give up gluten, I used to go to a certain seafood restaurant at least once a year, just so I could indulge in a basket of their cheddar-bay biscuits. I'm happy to say that my cheddar biscuits bear a striking resemblance to the originals.

One more craving satisfied!

Corn Muffins

1 cup milk
½ cup FAGE 2% Greek yogurt
¼ cup corn oil
1 large egg
½ teaspoon salt
1/3 cup brown sugar
2 teaspoons baking powder
½ cup Better Batter GF flour
¾ cup cornmeal
¾ cup blanched almond flour

Mix the milk, sour cream, egg, corn oil, sugar and salt till fluffy. Fold in the baking powder and Better Batter then mix for 2 minutes. Add the corn meal and almond flour then mix till blended.

Line muffin tins with paper liners and put 1/3 cup of batter into each section. Makes 12 muffins.

Bake at 350° for 22-25 minutes.

Chili Cheese Cornbread

¾ cup 2% FAGE Greek Yogurt
2 tablespoons corn oil
1 extra-large egg
¾ teaspoon salt
½ teaspoon garlic powder
2 tablespoons dark brown sugar
1 teaspoon California chili powder
2 teaspoons baking powder
½ teaspoon baking soda
½ cup Better Batter GF flour
¾ cup yellow corn meal
¾ cup blanched almond flour
2½ cups super sweet corn kernels
1 cup diced mild green chilies*
½ cup green onions finely sliced
6 ounces extra sharp cheddar cheese shredded

Combine the yogurt, egg, salt, garlic, chili powder and brown sugar then mix with an electric mixer till well blended. Add the Better Batter and mix on high for 1-2 minutes. Add the corn meal and almond flour and mix thoroughly. (At this point you may have to use a large spoon if it's too thick for the mixer) Mix in the green onions and green chilies. Fold in the corn and then the cheese.

Spread the batter in a 13X9 inch cake pan lined with parchment paper and oiled.

Bake at 375 ° for 50-60 minutes till golden brown.

Serve warm.

*For a milder taste substitute finely diced red bell pepper.

For a hearty meal serve with a bowl of black bean soup.

Cookies

No-Bake Orange Cookies

1/3 cup almond butter
½ cup frozen orange juice concentrate
1 teaspoon vanilla
A pinch of salt
1½ cups GF rolled oats
½ cup unsweetened shredded coconut
¼ cup dried currants
¼ cup blanched slivered almonds

In a sauce pan over medium heat combine the almond butter, concentrated orange juice and vanilla. Heat until simmering and then remove from heat and add the oats and coconut. Stir well to combine. Fold in the currants and almonds.

Working quickly, drop by tablespoonful onto a parchment or wax paper lined baking sheet. Press with the back of a spoon to make the cookies about the size of a silver dollar and about ½ inch thick. Allow to cool for at least 60 minutes prior to serving.

Refrigerate.

Variations:

Use a pinch each of cloves and allspice instead of the vanilla.

Add ¼ cup finely diced dried apricots instead of the currants.

Chocolate Chip Cookies

1 stick butter softened
¾ cup brown sugar
½ teaspoon salt
3 tablespoons water*
1 egg
1 teaspoon vanilla extract
½ cup Better Batter GF flour
½ teaspoon baking soda
1 cup blanched almond flour
1 cup semi-sweet chocolate chips

Cream the butter and sugar together. Add the salt, egg, vanilla and water then beat until fluffy. Fold in the Better Batter and baking soda then **beat for two minutes**. Fold in the almond flour then mix thoroughly. Fold in the chocolate chips.

Drop by tablespoonful onto parchment lined baking sheets.

Bake at 375° for 14-17 minutes until the cookies are golden brown.

Allow the cookies to cool for at least 20 minutes before removing them from cookie sheet.

Makes 24 cookies.

*These cookies are moist and chewy. For extra crisp cookies, use only 1 tablespoon of water.

Nut Cookies

1 stick butter
¾ cup brown sugar
2 eggs
1 teaspoon vanilla
1 tablespoon water
1/8 teaspoon salt
½ teaspoon baking soda
¼ cup Better Batter GF flour
½ cup blanched almond flour
¾ cup shredded unsweetened coconut
1 cup chopped pecans or walnuts

Mix melted butter, sugar, eggs, salt, vanilla and water till fluffy. Fold in the Better Batter and baking soda then mix for a minute or two until the batter thickens. Fold in the almond flour and mix till well blended. Fold in the remaining ingredients.

Drop by tablespoonful onto parchment-lined cookie sheets.

Bake at 350° 11-13 minutes

Allow the cookies to cool for at least 20 minutes before removing them from cookie sheet.

Makes 24 cookies.

Cranberry Spice Cookies

1 stick butter softened
¾ cup brown sugar
½ teaspoon salt
3 tablespoons water
1 egg
1 teaspoon orange extract
1/8 teaspoon allspice
1/16 teaspoon ground cloves
½ cup Better Batter GF flour
½ teaspoon baking soda
1 cup blanched almond flour
1 cup dried cranberries

Cream the butter and sugar together. Add the salt, egg, orange extract, water, allspice and cloves then beat until fluffy. Fold in the Better Batter and baking soda then **beat for two minutes**. Fold in the almond flour then mix thoroughly. Fold in the cranberries.

Drop by tablespoonful onto parchment lined baking sheets.

Bake at 375° for 15-17 minutes until the cookies are golden brown.

Allow the cookies to cool for at least 20 minutes before removing them from cookie sheet.

Makes 24 cookies.

White Chocolate and Macadamia Nut Cookies

1 stick butter softened
½ cup brown sugar
¼ cup white sugar
½ teaspoon salt
1 egg
2 tablespoons water
1 teaspoon vanilla
½ cup Better Batter GF flour
½ teaspoon baking soda
1 cup blanched almond flour
¾ cup GF white chocolate chips
½ cup chopped macadamia nuts

Cream the butter and sugar together. Add the salt, egg, water and vanilla then beat until fluffy. Fold in the Better Batter and baking soda then **beat for 2 minutes**. Fold in the almond flour then mix thoroughly. Fold in the chocolate chips and the nuts. Drop by tablespoonful onto parchment lined baking sheets.

Bake at 375° for 14-17 minutes until the cookies are golden brown.

Allow the cookies to cool for at least 20 minutes before removing them from cookie sheet.

Makes 24 cookies.

Everything Cookies

1 stick butter
¾ cup brown sugar
2 eggs
1 teaspoon vanilla
¼ teaspoon salt
1 tablespoon Better Batter GF flour
½ teaspoon baking soda
¾ cup blanched almond flour
1 cup gluten free rolled oats
½ cup unsweetened grated coconut
1 cup dried currants
1 cup semi-sweet chocolate chips
1 cup walnuts broken into small pieces

Beat the butter and sugar until fluffy. Add the eggs, vanilla and salt and continue to mix. Fold in the Better Batter and soda then mix for a minute. Fold in the almond flour then mix thoroughly. Mix in the oats then fold in the remaining ingredients.

Drop onto cookie parchment lined cookie sheets.

Bake at 350 ° for 11-13 minutes until they are golden brown.

Allow the cookies to cool for at least 20 minutes before removing them from cookie sheet.

Makes 24 cookies.

Double Chocolate Cookies

1 stick butter
¾ cup brown sugar
¼ teaspoon salt
¼ cup sour cream
1 egg
1 teaspoon vanilla
2 teaspoons instant (decaffeinated) coffee
1 tablespoon Kailua (or water)
¼ cup Ghirardelli ground sweet chocolate and coco powder
¼ cup + 1 tablespoon Ghirardelli unsweetened coco powder
½ teaspoon baking soda
2 tablespoons Better Batter GF flour
1½ cups blanched almond flour
1½ cups chocolate chips *(I use Ghirardelli 60%)*
2 cups walnuts broken into large chunks

Cream together the butter and sugar and salt. Add the egg, vanilla and sour cream. Dissolve the coffee in the Kailua and add to the mixture then whip until the mixture is light and fluffy. Fold in the cocoa powder then mix thoroughly. Fold in the Better Batter and baking soda then mix for two minutes. Fold in the almond flour then mix. Fold in the chocolate chips and nuts.

Drop by heaping tablespoon onto two baking sheets lined with parchment paper.

Bake at 350 for 14-18 minutes

Allow the cookies to cool for at least 20 minutes before removing them from cookie sheet.

These cookies are intensely chocolate, crunchy on the outside and chewy on the inside.

Lemon Thins

1 stick butter
¾ cup sugar
1 egg
5 tablespoons freshly squeezed lemon juice
¼ teaspoon salt
¼ teaspoon baking powder
½ cup Better Batter GF flour
¾ cup blanched almond flour
Zest of 2 lemons

Beat the butter, sugar, eggs and salt till fluffy. Fold in the Better Batter and baking powder then beat for another minute. Fold in the almond flour and beat until well mixed. Fold in the lemon zest.

Drop by rounded teaspoon onto parchment paper lined baking sheets.

Bake at 375° for 10-15 minutes till just brown around the edges.

Makes 28-30 cookies.

Sesame Shortbreads

1 stick butter
1/3 cup + 1 tablespoon sugar
¼ teaspoon salt
½ cup Better Batter GF flour
1/3 cup blanched almond flour
¼ cup sesame seeds
½ cup finely shredded unsweetened coconut

Cream the butter, sugar and salt till fluffy. Fold in the Better Batter then mix for a minute. Fold in the almond flour then mix till completely blended. Fold in the sesame seeds and coconut.

Turn the mixture onto a sheet of wax paper and form it into a log about 1½ inches in diameter. Roll the dough in the wax paper, place it in a plastic bag and refrigerate for about 2 hours till it's firm. **Do not freeze.**

Slice the dough into ¼ inch thick rounds and place the slices at least 2 inches apart on parchment lined cookie sheets.

Bake at 325° for 15-25 minutes till they are golden brown.

Allow the cookies to cool on the cookie sheets. They are quite fragile till cool.

Makes 24 cookies.

Thumb Print Cookies

1 stick unsalted butter
4 ounces cream cheese
½ cup sugar
1 egg
½ teaspoon vanilla extract
½ cup + 1 tablespoon Better Batter GF flour
1 cup blanched almond flour
Seedless raspberry jam

Cream the butter, sugar and egg together until fluffy. Beat in the vanilla. Fold in the Better Batter then mix for a minute. Fold in the almond flour and mix till well blended.

Refrigerate for at least 30 minutes.

Drop by rounded spoonful onto a cookie sheet lined with parchment paper. Press your thumb gently into the center of each cookie to form a shallow well. Put a scant half teaspoon of jam into the center of each cookie.

Bake at 350° for 17-20 minutes till just golden on the bottom

Cool before eating

Makes 24 cookies.

Variations: Use apricot preserves or Nutella instead of the raspberry jam.

Pignoli Cookies

12 ounces blanched slivered almonds
¼ teaspoon salt
2 cups powdered sugar
2 teaspoons almond extract
4 egg whites
2 cups pine nuts

Whirl the almonds and salt in a food processor until they turn into a paste. Add the sugar and pulse to combine. Add the almond extract and **2** egg whites then whirl until a doughy ball forms.

Turn the dough onto a plate, knead it together and then form a log. Divide it in half and then each half into fourths. Finally cut each piece into four pieces.

Put the 2 remaining egg whites into a small bowl and the pine nuts into a second bowl.

Roll each piece of dough in in your hands to form a ball then dip it in the egg whites. Finally, press the ball into the pine nuts, put more nuts on top and press them into the dough forming a cookie about ½ inch thick.

Arrange the cookies at least an inch apart on parchment lined cookie sheets.

Bake at 325° for 16-20 minutes until the cookies are golden. Allow the cookies to cool in the pan.

Makes 32 cookies

Rugelach

Dough:
1 cup Better Batter GF flour
1¼ cups blanched almond flour
¼ teaspoon salt
1 tablespoon sugar
1 stick very cold butter
4 ounces cream cheese
¼ cup sour cream
1-2 tablespoons cold water
Extra almond flour for rolling out the dough

Filling:
¾ cups finely chopped walnuts
1/3 cup dark brown sugar
Optional: ½ teaspoon cinnamon

For the dough: Place all the dry ingredients in the food processor and pulse until well blended. Cut the butter into cubes and add to the dry ingredients then pulse a couple times until it forms coarse grains. Cut the cream cheese into cubes. Add the cream cheese and sour cream and pulse till mixed. Add the water and pulse for a few seconds till a dough begins to form.

Turn the dough onto a plate, divide it into fourths and Knead each one just enough to form a ball. Wrap each ball of dough in plastic wrap and refrigerate for several hours or overnight.

For the filling: Combine the ingredients in a small bowl

To assemble: Take one ball of dough at a time out of the refrigerator. Dust the outside with almond flour and sprinkle more on the parchment paper you are going to roll the dough on. Roll between 2 sheets of parchment paper till you have a nine-inch diameter circle. Use a sharp knife to gently remove any ragged edges then cut the dough into twelve triangles. Sprinkle the dough with the sugar and nut mixture.

Beginning at the wide end, gently roll each triangle to form a crescent. Refrigerate the cookies while you repeat the process with each ball of dough.

Arrange the cookies on parchment lined cookie sheets, brush with egg wash just before baking.

Bake at 350° for 20 – 25 minutes till they are golden brown.

Optional: Sprinkle finely diced dried apricots, a few dried currants or some mini chocolate chips on top of the sugar mixture before rolling.

Apricot Scones

1½ cups blanched almond flour
1 cup Better Batter GF flour
¼ cup sugar
1 teaspoon baking powder
1 teaspoon baking soda
½ teaspoon salt
¾ cup dried apricots finely chopped
1 stick butter – diced and very cold
1 teaspoon vanilla
½ cup Fage 2% Greek yogurt
1 egg
1 tablespoon milk
2-3 tablespoons coarse turbinado sugar

In a food processor, pulse the flours, sugar, soda, baking powder and salt till well mixed. Add the apricots and pulse again till they are coated with flour. Add the butter bits and pulse till coarse crumbles form. Mix the egg, yogurt and vanilla together then add the mixture to the food processor. Pulse till a chunky dough forms. You should see pea-size bits of butter throughout the dough.

Turn the dough onto a plate and knead till it just sticks together. Divide the dough in half. Form two disks about seven inches diameter and ¾ inch thick.

Wrap the dough in plastic wrap and refrigerate for at least an hour.

Place the rounds of dough on a parchment lined cookie sheet. Brush each round with milk and then sprinkle the top with course sugar. Wet a long knife in hot water then wipe it dry. Cut each round in half and then each half into thirds. Separate the pieces so there's about a half inch of space between the wedges.

Bake at 400° 20-25 minutes
The scones should be golden brown.

Variations: Instead of apricots, you can substitute dried, tart cherries, dried blueberries, dried cranberries or mini chocolate chips (or any combination).

Fresh berries will NOT work with this recipe. There would be too much moisture.

Cherry Chocolate Chip Scones

6 tablespoons butter - frozen
1 cup Better Batter GF flour
1 cup blanched almond flour
¼ cup sugar
2 teaspoons baking powder
½ teaspoon baking soda
¾ teaspoon salt
¾ cup dried tart cherries
½ cup mini chocolate chips
½ cup + 2 tablespoons Fage 2% Greek yogurt
3 tablespoons cream
1-2 tablespoons coarse Turbinado sugar

Grate the butter on the coarse side of a box grater then put it in the freezer while you prepare the rest of the ingredients.

Mix all the dry ingredients in a large bowl till they are thoroughly blended. Toss in the cherries and chocolate chips then mix till they are well distributed and coated with flour. Fold in the grated butter with a fork till you have coarse crumbs. **Add 2 tablespoons of cream** in small bits as you turn over the dry mixture.

Knead three or four times then the divide the dough into halves. Form each half into a flat disc about seven inches in diameter.

Wrap the dough in plastic wrap and refrigerate for at least an hour.

Place the rounds of dough on a parchment lined cookie sheet. Brush each round with cream and then sprinkle the top with course sugar. Wet a long knife in hot water then wipe it dry. Cut each round in half and then each half into thirds. Separate the pieces so there's about a half inch of space between the wedges.

Bake at 400° for 20-25 minutes or until just golden and done in the center.

Separate the triangles while they are still warm

I have chosen to include two scone recipes because both are wonderful, but also because this version does not require a food processor. It presents a different method of incorporating the butter that you could also use for biscuits and pastry dough.

Brownies

1 cup Ghirardelli 60% chocolate chips (5 ounces)
1 stick butter
¾ cup sugar
3 eggs
¼ teaspoon salt
1½ teaspoons vanilla
2 teaspoons instant coffee (I use decaf)
½ cup Fage 2% Greek yogurt*
¼ cup unsweetened cocoa powder
1/3 cup Better Batter GF flour
1 teaspoon baking powder
½ cup blanched almond flour
2 cups walnuts broken into pieces
A generous pat of butter for the pan

Place the chocolate chips in a microwave safe bowl and microwave on high for 30 seconds. Let them sit for a minute then stir the chocolate. If it's not melted, microwave for another 30 seconds, wait a minute or two then stir again. Repeat the cycle until MOST of the chips are melted then stir to melt the rest. Set aside.

In a large bowl beat the butter and sugar with an electric mixer till fluffy. Add the eggs and salt and continue mixing till the mixture is pale yellow and fluffy. Dissolve the coffee in the vanilla then add it along with the yogurt to the batter and mix. Add the melted chocolate and mix till well blended. Fold in the cocoa powder then mix till well blended. Fold in the Better Batter and baking powder and mix for a minute or two until the mixture begins to thicken.

156

Fold in the almond flour and mix till completely combined. Fold in the nuts.

Butter the bottom and sides of a 13 X 9 inch **nonstick** cake pan. (If you don't have nonstick, use buttered parchment paper on the bottom and sides.)

The mixture will be quite thick so drop it into the pan by large spoonful to get it fairly well distributed then use a rubber spatula to spread it evenly in the pan.

Bake on the second to bottom rack at 325° for 35-45 minutes.
Test doneness with a toothpick.

Separate the sides from the pan with a plastic spatula BEFORE the brownies cool. Use a sharp knife to cut the TOP of the brownies then use a spatula to cut down to the bottom so you don't damage your pan.

For more cake-like brownies, use 2/3 cup yogurt.

Cakes and Muffins

Blueberry Muffins

1 stick butter
1 cup light brown sugar
¼ teaspoon salt
3 eggs
½ cup + 2 tablespoons Fage 2% Greek yogurt
1½ teaspoons vanilla
1½ teaspoons baking powder
¾ cup Better Batter GF flour
¾ cup blanched almond flour
1¾ cups fresh blueberries
1 tablespoon coarse Turbinado sugar

Whip the softened butter, sugar, salt, eggs and yogurt and vanilla till fluffy. Fold in the Better Batter and baking powder then beat for 2 minutes. Fold in the almond flour then mix till thoroughly blended. (The mixture will be very thick.) Fold in the blueberries.

Line muffin tins with paper liners and put 1/3 cup of batter into each section. Sprinkle the top of each muffin with a pinch of Turbinado sugar.

Bake at 350° for 28-35 minutes.

Allow the muffins to sit in the pans for a few minutes before removing them.

Makes 15 muffins

Banana Blueberry Muffins

2 eggs
2 tablespoons corn oil
2 tablespoons brown sugar
1 teaspoon vanilla
4 ripe bananas mashed
2 tablespoons Better Batter GF flour
1 cup blanched almond flour
¼ teaspoon salt
¾ teaspoon baking soda
½ cup unsweetened dried blueberries
1 cup walnut chunks

Mix the eggs, oil, sugar, salt and vanilla together. Add the bananas and mix till well blended. Fold in the Better Batter and baking soda then mix for 2 minutes. Fold in the almond flour and mix until blended. Fold in the berries and nuts.

Line muffin tins with paper liners and put 1/3 cup of batter into each section.

Bake at 350° for 30-35 minutes

Test for doneness by inserting a dry toothpick into the center of one muffin.

Makes 12 muffins

Banana Chocolate Chip Muffins

3 eggs
3 tablespoons corn oil
3 tablespoons brown sugar
1 teaspoon vanilla
¼ teaspoon salt
4 very ripe bananas mashed
3 tablespoons Better Batter GF flour
¾ teaspoon baking soda
1 cup blanched almond flour
1 cup semi-sweet chocolate chips
2 ounces 87% chocolate chopped

Mix the eggs, oil, brown sugar, vanilla and salt till fluffy. Add the bananas and continue to mix. Fold in the Better Batter and baking soda then mix for 2 minutes. Fold in the almond flour and mix thoroughly. Fold in the chocolate.

Line muffin tins with paper liners and put 1/3 cup of batter into each section.

Bake at 350° for 32-37 minutes
Test for doneness by inserting a dry toothpick into the center of one muffin.

Makes 15 muffins

These muffins are dense, moist and have a texture similar to bread pudding. They're best served slightly warm so the chocolate is still gooey.

Cranberry Nut Muffins

¾ cup brown sugar
2 eggs
1/3 cup orange juice or water*
Optional: *Replace 2 tablespoons of the water or juice with Grand Marnier.
1 teaspoon orange extract
¼ cup corn oil
1/8 teaspoon allspice
1/16 teaspoon ground cloves
¼ teaspoon salt
1 teaspoon baking powder
½ cup + 1 tablespoon Better Batter GF flour
½ cup + 1 tablespoon blanched almond flour
Zest of one orange
8 ounces fresh cranberries roughly chopped
2 cups walnuts broken into pieces

Combine the sugar, eggs, oil, water, spices and salt and beat till fluffy. Fold in the Better Batter and baking powder then mix for 2 minutes. Fold in the almond flour then mix till well combined. Fold in the nuts and cranberries.

Line muffin tins with paper liners then put 1/3 cup of batter into each section.

Bake at 350° for 28-30 minutes
The muffins are done when they are golden brown and spring back when touched with a finger.

Makes 12 muffins

Variation: add ½ cup finely diced dried apricots.

Serve with cream cheese whipped with a little orange marmalade or top with an orange glaze.

Butter Pecan Muffins

1 stick butter
1 cup brown sugar
¼ teaspoon salt
3 eggs
½ cup + 2 Tablespoons Fage 2% Greek yogurt
1½ teaspoons vanilla
1½ teaspoons baking powder
¾ cups Better Batter GF flour
¾ cup blanched almond flour
1 cup chopped pecans

Beat the softened butter, sugar, salt, eggs, yogurt and vanilla till fluffy. Fold in the Better Batter and baking powder then beat for 1-2 minutes until the mixture thickens. Fold in the almond flour then mix till blended. (The mixture will be very thick.) Fold in the nuts.

Line muffin tins with paper liners and put 1/3 cup of batter into each section.

Bake at 350° for 28-32 minutes

Makes 12 muffins

Streusel Topped Orange Muffins

1 cup light brown sugar
1 stick butter
¼ teaspoon salt
3eggs
½ cup frozen orange juice concentrate (thawed)
2 tablespoons Grand Marnier Liqueur
½ teaspoon orange extract
1 teaspoon vanilla
1½ teaspoons baking powder
3/4 cup Better Batter GF flour
3/4 cup blanched almond flour

Topping:
½ stick butter
¼ cup Better Batter GF flour mix
½ cup blanched almond flour
½ cup dark brown sugar
½ teaspoon vanilla

Batter: Combine the sugar, butter, salt and eggs then beat till fluffy. Mix in the remaining wet ingredients. Fold in the baking powder and Better Batter then beat for a minute or two till the mixture thickens. Fold in the almond flour then mix till smooth. Fold in the orange zest.

Topping: Mix the dry ingredients till well blended then cut in the softened butter with a fork until the mixture is crumbly. Drizzle in the vanilla and continue to mix.

Line muffin tins with paper liners then put ¼ cup of batter into each section. Divide the streusel topping evenly over the batter, about 2 teaspoons each.

Bake at 350° for 25-28 minutes
Test for doneness with a toothpick.

Gently push any topping that has run over onto the pan back on the muffins as soon as they come out of the oven. Allow the muffins to cool in the tins before gently lifting them out.

Makes 15 muffins

Variation: instead of vanilla, substitute ½ teaspoon cinnamon in the streusel topping.

To make a layer cake
Make a double recipe of batter.

Line the bottoms of two 8 inch nonstick cake pans with parchment paper then generously butter the bottom and sides. Divide the batter equally between the two pans then smooth the tops with a rubber spatula.

Bake at 350° for 30-40 minutes

Allow the cakes to cool in the pans for 20-30 minutes before turning them out.

Frost with chocolate buttercream icing, cream cheese icing or a dark chocolate ganache.

Chocolate Buttercream

1½ sticks butter
¼ teaspoon salt
2 cups powdered sugar
1 teaspoon vanilla
½ cup + 2 tablespoons coco powder
½ cup + 2 tablespoons heavy cream

Let the butter come to room temperature. In a large bowl combine the butter, salt, sugar, vanilla and coco powder. Begin mixing on low with an electric mixer and slowly add half the cream. When the ingredients are moist, turn the mixer up to high power. Add the remaining cream, a little at a time as you continue to whip the mixture until your frosting is the texture of thick whipped cream. (4-5 minutes)

Dark Chocolate Ganache

1 cup heavy cream
1 cup 60% chocolate chips
¼ cup sugar
1 teaspoon instant coffee

Bring the cream to a simmer in a saucepan then remove it from the heat and add the remaining ingredients. Stir until the chocolate is completely melted and the mixture is smooth then refrigerate for a half hour. Stir then pour it over the center of the cake, it will run to the edges. Don't pour on the ganache until it has had time to thicken a little. It's not fun to clean up!

Lemon Muffins

1 cup sugar
1 stick butter
¼ teaspoon salt
3 eggs
1/2 cup+ 2 tablespoons lemon juice
3 tablespoons lemon zest (from 3-4 lemons)
1 teaspoon vanilla
1½ teaspoons baking powder
3/4 cup Better Batter GF flour
3/4 cup blanched almond flour

Syrup:
2/3 cup sugar
¼ cup lemon juice

Combine the sugar, butter and salt then beat till fluffy. Add the lemon juice and vanilla then beat to combine. Fold in the baking powder and Better Batter then beat for a minute or two till the mixture thickens. Fold in the almond flour and mix till smooth. Fold in the lemon zest.

Line muffin tins with paper liners then put 1/3 cup of batter into each cup.

Bake at 350° for 26-29 minutes.

Turn muffins out of the pan and spoon the syrup over them as soon as they're out of the oven.

Makes 11 muffins

To make a cake:

Place a piece of parchment paper over the bottom of an 8 inch spring form pan then clamp on the side. Generously butter the bottom and sides then spoon the batter into the pan and smooth the top with a spatula.

Place the pan on a cookie sheet in case it leaks.

Bake at 350° for 35-45 minutes.

Allow the cake to cool in the pan for 15-20 minutes then transfer it to a cake plate.

Pour the syrup over the top of the cake a little at a time so it has time to soak in.

This cake is tart, sweet and so moist it resembles a bread pudding in texture.

Garnish with fresh raspberries or a raspberry coulis.

Yellow Cupcakes

1 cup white sugar
½ cup corn oil
¼ teaspoon salt
3 eggs
½ cup + 2 tablespoons Fage 2% Greek yogurt
1½ teaspoons vanilla
1½ teaspoons baking powder
1 cup blanched almond flour
½ cup Better Batter GF flour

Beat the sugar, oil, salt and eggs together till fluffy. Add the yogurt and vanilla then beat till combined. Fold in the Better Batter and baking powder then beat for a minute or two until the mixture thickens. Fold in the almond flour and mix till well combined.

Line muffin tins with paper liners then put 1/3 cup of batter into each section.

Bake at 350° for 26-31 minutes.
Test for doneness with a toothpick.

Makes 12 cupcakes

To make a cake: Line the bottom of a nine-inch, nonstick cake pan with parchment paper then generously butter the bottom and sides. Spoon in the batter then smooth with a rubber spatula.

Bake at 350° for 33-45 minutes.

Test for doneness with a toothpick.

Chocolate Fudge Cupcakes

½ stick butter
1 cup white sugar
3 eggs
½ cup sour cream
½ cup Fage 2% Greek yogurt
2 teaspoons instant coffee
2 tablespoons Kailua
1 teaspoon vanilla
¼ teaspoon salt
1½ teaspoons baking powder
½ cup Ghirardelli unsweetened cocoa powder
¼ cup Ghirardelli ground sweet chocolate and cocoa
1/3 cup Better Batter GF flour
1 cup blanched almond flour
1/3 cup chocolate chips

Mix the softened butter, sugar, eggs, sour cream, yogurt, vanilla and salt till light and fluffy. Dissolve the coffee in the Kailua then add it to the mixture. Fold in the coco powder then mix for a minute. Fold in the Better Batter and baking powder then mix until the batter begins to thicken. Fold in the almond flour and mix till thoroughly combined.

Line cupcake tins with paper liners then put 1/3 cup of batter into each section.

Bake at 350 for 28-34 minutes
Test for doneness with a toothpick.

Makes 16 cupcakes

Leave the cupcakes in the baking pan for two or three minutes then carefully remove them and place them on an oven safe plate. Immediately put six or seven chocolate chips on top of each cupcake then place them in the oven **which has been turned off** for about 20 seconds. Return the plates to the counter top. Spread the melted chocolate with a butter knife to "ice" the cupcakes.

These cupcakes are moist and intensely chocolate. They're a favorite wherever I take them!

To make a cake:

Line the bottom of two 8 inch nonstick cake pans with parchment paper then generously butter the bottom and sides. Divide the batter between the pans and smooth with a rubber spatula.

Bake at 350° for 37-47 minutes

Allow them to cool in the pans for 20-30 minutes before turning them out.

Frost with dark a chocolate ganache or a mocha cream cheese frosting.

173

Black Forest Cupcakes

½ stick butter
1 cup white sugar
3 eggs
½ cup sour cream
½ cup Fage 2% Greek yogurt
2 teaspoons instant coffee
2 tablespoons Kailua
1 teaspoon vanilla
¼ teaspoon salt
1 teaspoon baking powder
½ cup Ghirardelli unsweetened cocoa powder
¼ cup Ghirardelli ground sweet chocolate and cocoa
1/3 cup Better Batter GF flour
1 cup blanched almond flour
1 can "more fruit" cherry pie filling
1/3 cup chocolate chips

Mix the melted butter, sugar, eggs, sour cream, yogurt, vanilla and salt till light and fluffy. Dissolve the coffee in the Kailua and add it to the mixture. Fold in the coco powders then mix for a minute. Fold in the Better Batter, soda and baking powder then mix until the batter begins to thicken, about 2 minutes. Fold in the almond flour and mix till thoroughly combined.

Line muffin tins with paper liners and put ¼ cup of batter into each section. Top each cupcake with one tablespoon cherry pie filling.

Bake at 350° for 28-33 minutes.

Test for doneness with a toothpick.

Makes 20 cupcakes

When they are cool enough to handle, remove the cupcakes from the pan.

Put the chocolate chips in a heat safe dish and set it in the still warm oven that has been turned off for 15-30 seconds. Stir. If the chocolate is still not melted, return it to the oven for another 15-30 seconds.

Put the melted chocolate in a zip lock bag. Cut a TINY tip off one corner. Squeeze a thin, wavy line of chocolate over the top of each cupcake.

German Chocolate Cupcakes

3 eggs - separated
1 stick butter
1 cup sugar
½ cup + 2 tablespoons Fage 2% Greek yogurt
¼ teaspoon salt
1 teaspoon vanilla
2 ounces German sweet chocolate
2 tablespoons water
1 tablespoon unsweetened cocoa powder
½ teaspoon baking soda
½ teaspoon baking powder
½ cup Better Batter gluten free flour
1 cup blanched almond flour

Coconut Pecan Frosting (recipe follows)

Separate the eggs. Put the whites in a bowl large enough to whip them in and the yolks in any small bowl.

Break the chocolate into small pieces and place in a bowl with 2 tablespoons water. Microwave till the chocolate is just melted. (about 60 seconds at 30%)

Beat the butter and sugar till fluffy. Add the yogurt, vanilla and salt and beat till fluffy. Add the egg yolks and mix for another 30 seconds. Mix the chocolate and water with a spoon till you're sure it's completely melted then add it to the mixture and mix thoroughly. Fold in the Better Batter, cocoa powder, baking soda and baking powder and **mix**

for 2 minutes, till the mixture thickens. Fold in the almond flour then mix till well blended.

Whip the egg whites into stiff peaks. Add about a third of the egg whites to the batter and mix with a spoon to lighten the mixture. Carefully fold the remaining egg whites into the batter.

Line muffin tins with paper liners and put ¼ cup of batter into each section.

Bake at 350° for 28-31 minutes

Makes 16 cupcakes.

If the cupcakes have run over at all, immediately push the edges away from the pan with the back of a butter knife. If it cools, it's almost impossible to unstick the edges without breaking the cupcakes.

Place them on a rack to cool.

Coconut Pecan Frosting

2 egg yolks
¾ cup evaporated milk
1 teaspoon vanilla
¼ teaspoon salt
2/3 cup sugar
1½ sticks butter
1 cup unsweetened grated coconut
1 cup coarsely chopped pecans

Melt the butter. Whisk in the milk, and egg yolks. Whisk in the sugar and begin to warm the mixture over **low** heat stirring constantly until it begins to thicken and takes on a light caramel color. Add the coconut and cook for another minute then fold in the nuts and set aside to cool.

When the cupcakes and icing are cool, Mound a heaping tablespoon of icing on top of each cupcake. (It's too thick to spread)

If you are going to keep them longer than a couple of hours, they should be refrigerated.

Spiced Cran-Apple Pandowdy

For the cake:
1 stick butter
½ cup dark brown sugar
¼ teaspoon salt
3 eggs
½ cup Fage 2% Greek yogurt
1½ teaspoons vanilla
1½ teaspoons baking powder
½ cup Better Batter GF flour
1¼ cups blanched almond flour
Butter for the pan

Whip the softened butter, sugar, salt, eggs, yogurt and vanilla till fluffy. Fold in the Better Batter and baking powder then whip for a minute or two till the mixture thickens. Fold in the almond flour and mix till thoroughly blended. (The mixture will be very thick.)

For the fruit topping:
5 apples peeled and cut into ½ inch dice (about 6 cups)
Juice of half a lemon
½ cup fresh cranberries sliced in half
1/3 cup dark brown sugar
1 tablespoon Better Batter GF flour
1/16 teaspoon ground allspice
1/16 teaspoon ground cloves
2 tablespoons Butter

Put the brown sugar, Better Batter, cloves and allspice into a gallon size plastic bag and shake to mix thoroughly.

Squeeze the lemon juice over the diced apples and cranberries then drop them into the bag and shake until they are evenly coated with the sugar and spice mixture.

Butter the bottom and sides of a 9X9 inch nonstick pan.
Evenly distribute the fruit mixture on the bottom of the pan. Dot the fruit with 2 tablespoons of butter.

Spread the batter evenly on top of the fruit. It's very thick so the easiest way is to spoon it over the top and then level it with the back of the spoon or a rubber spatula.

Bake at 350° for 40 – 45 minutes (The top will be very brown.)
Test for doneness with a toothpick

While the cake is still warm, go around the sides with a spatula to loosen it from the pan then it onto a serving plate.

If you are going to use an 8X8 pan, there will be too much batter to cook properly, so put about a cup of the fruit mixture and the ¾ cup of batter into a 3X5 inch buttered mini loaf pan.

The recipe will also make 5 mini loaves.

Cherry Coffee Cake
with Streusel Topping

1 stick butter
½ cup dark brown sugar
¼ teaspoon salt
3 eggs
½ cup Fage 2% Greek yogurt
1½ teaspoons vanilla
1½ teaspoons baking powder
½ cup Better Batter GF flour
1¼ cups blanched almond flour
1 cup dried TART cherries

2 cans of extra fruit cherry pie filling

Beat the softened butter, sugar, salt, eggs, yogurt and vanilla till fluffy. Fold in the Better Batter and baking powder then mix for 1-2 minutes until the mixture begins to thicken. Fold in the almond flour and mix till blended. Fold in the dried cherries. *(The mixture will be quite thick.)*

To prepare a nine-inch non-stick spring form pan: Before assembling the pan place a sheet of parchment paper over the bottom then clamp on the rim of the pan. Trim the paper where it is sticking out of the pan. Generously butter the bottom and sides of the pan.

Spread the mixture evenly over the bottom of the prepared pan.

Top the batter with the cherry pie filling. I spoon out the cherries with just enough of the sauce to cover them which leaves about ¼ can of sweet sauce to throw away from each can.

Sprinkle the streusel topping evenly over the top of the pie filling.

Streusel Topping

½ stick butter
¼ cup better batter GF flour
½ cup almond flour
½ teaspoon vanilla
A dash of salt

Mix all the dry ingredients till well blended then cut in the softened butter with a fork until the mixture is crumbly. Drizzle in the vanilla and continue to mix.

Bake at 350° for 55-60 minutes

There's no accurate way to test for doneness because of the cherry pie topping so I bake it until the streusel topping is browned. It always seems to come out perfectly.

Allow the cake to cool completely then gently run a sharp knife around the edge to loosen the topping before removing the sides of the pan.

Vanilla Cheesecake

16 ounces cream cheese
2 eggs
¾ cup sugar
¾ cup sour cream
1 teaspoon vanilla*
Zest of 1 lemon

Topping
1½ cups sour cream
2 tablespoons sugar

1 graham cracker crust (recipe follows)

Allow the cream cheese to come to room temperature. Using an electric mixer combine the cream cheese, eggs, sugar, sour cream and vanilla. **Do NOT whip in a lot of air or the cheesecake or will crack.** Fold in the lemon zest. Pour into a pre-baked crust.

Bake at 350° for 35-40 minutes
When only a small area of the center jiggles when you gently nudge the pan, remove it from the oven, pour on the topping.
Bake for another 8 minutes.

Chill before serving.

*for more intense flavor, use a real vanilla bean.

Graham Cracker Crust

2 cups GF graham cracker crumbs
1 tablespoon sugar
1 stick of butter - melted

Combine the graham cracker crumbs and sugar then add the butter and mix till the crumbs are well coated. Press into a nonstick pie pan.

Bake at 325° for 10 minutes.

Kailua and Coffee Cheesecake

16 ounces cream cheese
2 eggs
½ cup sugar
½ cup sour cream
2 teaspoons instant coffee
1/3 cup Kailua Liqueur

Topping
1½ cups sour cream
2 tablespoons sugar

1 chocolate crust (recipe follows)

Allow the cream cheese to come to room temperature. Using an electric mixer combine the cream cheese, eggs, sugar and sour cream. Dissolve the instant coffee in the Kailua and add it to the batter. **Do NOT whip in a lot of air or the cheesecake will crack.**

Pour into a pre-baked chocolate crust.

Bake at 350° for 35-40 minutes.

When only a small area of the center jiggles when you gently nudge the pan, remove it from the oven, pour on the topping.

Bake for another 8 minutes.

Chill before serving.

185

Chocolate Crust

1½ cups blanched almond flour
¼ cup sugar
3 tablespoons coco powder
¾ stick butter melted

Combine all the ingredients until a dough forms. Press the dough into a nonstick pie pan.

Bake at 325°for 10-12 minutes.
Allow to cool before adding the filling.

Grand Marnier Cheese Cake

16 ounces cream cheese
2 eggs
½ cup sugar
½ cup sour cream
1 teaspoon orange extract
1/3 cup Grand Marnier Liqueur

Topping
1½ cups sour cream
2 tablespoons sugar

1 chocolate cookie crumb crust (recipe follows)

Allow the cream cheese to come to room temperature. Using an electric mixer combine the cream cheese, eggs, sugar and sour cream and orange extract. Add the Grand Marnier. **Do NOT whip in a lot of air or the cheesecake will crack.**

Pour into a pre-baked chocolate crust.

Bake at 350° for 35-40 minutes

When only a small area of the center jiggles when you gently nudge the pan, remove it from the oven, pour on the topping.

Bake for 8 more minutes.
Chill before serving.

Chocolate Cookie Crumb Crust

3 cups of GF chocolate cookies
1 stick of butter - melted

Crush the cookies into fine crumbs. (You should end up with 2 cups of crumbs. If you don't, crush more cookies.) Add the butter and mix till the crumbs are well coated. Press into a nonstick pie pan.

Bake at 325° for 10 minutes.

Tiramisu

For the cake:
1 stick butter
½ cup dark brown sugar
¼ teaspoon salt
3 eggs
½ cup Fage 2% Greek yogurt
1½ teaspoons vanilla
1½ teaspoons baking powder
½ cup Better Batter GF flour
1¼ cups blanched almond flour
Butter for the pan

For the Syrup:
½ cup brewed espresso
¼ cup Kailua

For the Topping:
8 ounces mascarpone cheese
1 cup heavy whipping cream
1 teaspoon vanilla
½ cup powdered sugar

1 ounce dark chocolate

Whip the softened butter, sugar, salt, eggs, yogurt and vanilla till fluffy. Fold in the Better Batter and baking powder then whip for a minute or two till the mixture thickens. Fold in the almond flour and mix till thoroughly blended. *(The mixture will be very thick.)*

Put parchment paper in the bottom of two eight inch round, nonstick cake pans then generously butter the bottom and sides. Divide the batter evenly between the 2 pans. *(The layers will be quite thin.)*

Bake at 350° for 15-25 minutes.

Allow the cakes to cool in the pans for 20 minutes then turn them out.

Combine the Coffee and Kailua. Using a pastry brush, soak the top of both layers of cake with the syrup. Then allow the cakes to cool completely.

Whip the mascarpone, cream, vanilla and sugar until the topping resembles very thick whipped cream. Spread a third of the mixture on one cake layer. Top with the second layer then spread the remaining topping on that layer. Grate the chocolate over the top.

Keep in the refrigerator.

Chocolate Decadence

1¼ cups heavy cream
10 ounce bag Ghirardelli 60% chocolate chips
3 heaping tablespoons seedless raspberry jam
2 tablespoons unsalted butter
Fresh or frozen raspberries to decorate

1 Chocolate crust (page 186)

Bring the cream to simmer in a sauce pan. Remove from heat then add the chocolate, butter and jam. Allow the mixture to sit for five minutes then stir until all the ingredients are completely melted and blended.

Pour into a large bowl. Refrigerate for 45 minutes then whip till there is a slight color change.

Pour into the pre-baked crust and refrigerate for at least 6 hours before serving.

Decorate with berries and whipped cream immediately before serving.

Whipped cream

¾ cup heavy cream
1 teaspoon vanilla
2 tablespoon sugar

Put all the ingredients in a large, **chilled** bowl and whip until stiff peaks form.

To make single serving desserts:

Line muffin tins with paper liners.

Put 1 teaspoon of crushed GF chocolate cookie crumbs in each cup then fill the cup with the chocolate-raspberry filling.

Refrigerate for several hours.

Top each serving with a half strawberry or several fresh raspberries.

Resources

My Favorite Sources for Ingredients

Blanched almond flour
nuts.com

Better Batter Gluten-Free All Purpose Flour
betterbatter.org
vitacost.com

Dried mushrooms
pistolrivermushrooms.com

Unsweetened coconut
nuts.com

Chickpea flour
nuts.com

Potato starch
nuts.com
vitacost.com
iherb.com

Gluten-Free Bouillon
Trader Joe's
Amazon.com

To see a photo gallery of food that was prepared
using recipes from this book please visit
www.JeriMillsMD.com

Jeri Mills is a physician, veterinarian, intuitive healer and avid home cook. When she learned that she could no longer eat gluten, she chose to view the situation as a creative challenge and set about re-creating all her favorite dishes in versions that were not only gluten-free, but as good as or better than the originals.

For years, she has shared her recipes with friends, colleagues and her patients. Now she is ready to share them with the world.

Her mission is to help everyone discover that Gluten-Free can be delicious!

Visit her on the web at

www.JeriMillsMD.com